THE
KENNEDY
LEGACY

ALSO BY JACQUES LOWE

Portrait: The Emergence of John F. Kennedy
Pacem in Terris
Persepolis: A Celebration
Kentucky: A Celebration of American Life
The Kennedy Years
Pilgrimage: Pope John Paul II in the Dominican Republic
Queen's Greatest Pix
The City: London's Financial Center
The Incredible Music Machine
Kennedy: A Time Remembered

———

ALSO BY WILFRID SHEED

Fiction

A Middle-Class Education
The Hack
Square's Progress
Office Politics
The Blacking Factory and Pennsylvania Gothic
Max Jamison
People Will Always Be Kind
Transatlantic Blues
The Boys of Winter

Nonfiction

The Morning After
Muhammad Ali
The Good Word
Clare Boothe Luce
Frank and Maisie: A Memoir with Parents

Anthologies

Sixteen Short Novels
G. K. Chesterton's Essays

THE
KENNEDY
LEGACY
—— A Generation Later ——

Photographs and Captions
by Jacques Lowe

Text by Wilfrid Sheed

Design by Ken Harris

VIKING
STUDIO
BOOKS

A
JACQUES LOWE
VISUAL ARTS PROJECTS
BOOK

VIKING STUDIO BOOKS
Published by the Penguin Group
Viking Penguin Inc., 40 West 23rd Street,
New York, New York 10010, U.S.A.
Penguin Books Ltd, 27 Wrights Lane,
London W8 5TZ, England
Penguin Books Australia Ltd, Ringwood,
Victoria, Australia
Penguin Books Canada Ltd, 2801 John Street,
Markham, Ontario, Canada L3R 1B4
Penguin Books (N. Z.) Ltd, 182–190 Wairau Road,
Auckland 10, New Zealand

Penguin Books Ltd, Registered Offices:
Harmondsworth, Middlesex, England

First published in the United States of America by Viking Penguin Inc. 1988
Published simultaneously in Canada
First published in Great Britain by Viking 1988

LIBRARY OF CONGRESS CATALOGING IN PUBLICATION DATA
Lowe, Jacques.
The Kennedy legacy.
1. Kennedy, John F. (John Fitzgerald), 1917–1963—
Influence. 2. Kennedy, Robert F., 1925–1968—Influence.
3. United States—History—1961–1969. I. Sheed, Wilfrid.
II. Title.
E842.1.L654   1988   973.922′092′2   87-29988
ISBN 0-670-81882-8

A CIP catalog record for this book is available from the British Library

Printed in the United States of America by Halliday Lithograph
Set in Electra and Trooper Roman

Contents

Introduction

This book—my part of it at least—might aptly be described as an act of "willed" memory. When my old friend and one-time colleague Jacques Lowe approached me with the idea of writing an essay about Jack Kennedy, I realized that my picture of the original had dimmed slightly, and that I couldn't remember exactly what I thought of him anymore. In recent years, several books had appeared, variously critical of Jack, and I had actually reviewed two of them myself.

I decided that what seemed to be missing from both the books I reviewed was a truly satisfying answer to the central question, Why were we so impressed at the time? Was our enthusiasm for Kennedy some sort of mass delusion based on a hoax? And when he died did we cry over nothing?

We have learned some new things about those years, although perhaps not as many as we think. For instance, Jack is much criticized these days for his covert military operations, but anyone paying attention knew about those operations, all right. In fact, one might almost say that no one did more than Jack to bring covert operations out of the closet, to which they have so messily returned. The subversions of Iran, Guatemala, and Chile occurred on other men's watches: insofar as it was possible in the murk of the Cold War, Kennedy preferred our positions made clear.

So perhaps the difference in our perception today is not altogether a matter of what we've learned but of what we've forgotten: the context seems to have disappeared. Bear in mind that by the late 1950s the Russians had just beaten us into space, had rolled into Hungary unopposed, and had even picked up a formidable ally in our own neighborhood in the person of Castro. In the circumstances, the next president *had* to be an activist, and Cold War ritual being what it is, the Russians *had* to test the hell out of him.

Thus, in 1961, Chairman Nikita Khrushchev announced a sweeping policy in support of insurrectionary wars everywhere, to which Kennedy had, in anticipation, already given his reply: a wrinkle of his own called "flexible response" or "limited war." With these ground rules set, much of what followed was inevitable, especially in Southeast Asia, where previous presidents had grandly offered to pick up the remaining chips of the old colonial powers, and play every last one to the bitter end.

In the continuum of the modern presidency, it takes some kind of miracle to change anything at all in under three years. But in parts of the world where he was freer to maneuver, such as Western Europe, Africa, India, and, most notably, South America, Kennedy either improved our relationships or, in the latter case, revolutionized them completely. And at home, he presided over a convulsive change in attitudes along a spectrum from civil rights on out to the sheer unthinkability of atomic weapons.

So all in all, most of us felt, as we sat glassy-eyed in front of our television sets that day, that Jack had done wonders with what he had been given, and that it had been a rare treat to watch him do it. This book is intended primarily as a reminder of just why we felt that way. And if Jack receives the benefit of the doubt once or twice, I can only say it's about time.

Anyway, that part of the assignment turned out to be a pleasure. Reliving the Jack Kennedy years was, for me and perhaps others, like reliving a particularly good period of one's own life. But Jacques also asked me to add an appreciation of Bobby Kennedy, and this I thought would be flat out impossible. As a die-hard Eugene McCarthy activist in 1968, I was still dying hard, and I could have sworn I would never find a good word to say for Bobby.

Then Jacques showed me the section of Cesar Chavez's oral history that refers to Bobby, and it was like a mist clearing from around a shadowy figure and revealing something quite unexpected: this was not, as we Eugenists had feared, some upstart pretending to be Jack but a potentially great man in his own right. Although his brother's name and memory may have helped Bobby to get his foot in various doors, from there on in he made an impression startlingly his own, and, in some cases, even stronger than Jack's.

Subsequently, my partner did a couple of interviews which show Bobby at work, and these, too, were eye-openers in their way. By 1966, the Bedford-Stuyvesant area of Brooklyn was considered a lost cause, a particularly gruesome example of the total breakdown of race relations in our cities. Yet Senator Bobby waded into this mess and somehow, working with whites and blacks together, helped to turn it around, making Bed-Stuy livable. Perhaps only a Kennedy could have had a chance to do it (the blacks had little time for other white men's names that year), and perhaps only Bobby could have done it so well.

When I once asked Ben Bradlee, a friend of both, to compare Jack with Bobby, he said that if the two of them had been presented to him as puzzles, Jack was the one he might have hoped to solve someday, Bobby never—so I probably wasn't the only one who failed to see the point of Bobby in his lifetime.

But subsequent investigation convinces me that Bobby may actually be the reason we can still talk seriously about a Kennedy legacy and not just a Kennedy presidency. By acting out, and improvising upon, Jack's proclaimed ideals of service, sacrifice, and compassion in the far less favorable climate of the later Johnson years, Bobby showed that his flag could be planted anytime, anyplace; you didn't need Jack's charm for the job anymore.

But it did take John F. Kennedy to climb the hill the first time.

■

ONE

The View from Abroad

In 1961–62, during the very heart of the Kennedy presidency, my young family and I had a magic chance to spend a whole year, summer to summer, in Europe—which we did, somewhat in England, mostly in Spain, and then camping back on out through France. You might suppose from this that we missed half the fun, but far from it. Europe turned out to be an excellent vantage point and echo chamber for taking in the Kennedy adventure.

The Paris edition of the *International Herald Tribune*—on such days as General Franco consented to allow it into the country—provided all the gossip you could reasonably wish (as any traveler can tell you, one small item from home in that excellent paper reverberates more richly than a full spread when you get back): but beyond that, one picked up something that stay-at-homes may have missed altogether: a sense that just for once the rest of the world approved of us and our choice.

Senator Kennedy and his new wife, the former Jacqueline Bouvier, work together at the senator's Capitol Hill office. The year is 1958 and JFK has just won a landslide reelection victory in his home state.

We had, against all expectation, actually picked a fellow human, a man whom even the French had no trouble respecting.

It is frequently said that Ronald Reagan has made Americans feel good about themselves—which many outsiders might not consider much of a trick; Kennedy pulled off the infinitely more difficult one of making other people feel good about us, too. Item: a bristly, tart sort of expatriate Englishman—the type from whose opinions one usually flinches even before he utters them—confided in me that Americans were far and away his favorite tourists: more curious, tolerant, and good-natured than anything bloody Europe had to offer these days. It's funny; we had never seemed that way before. (Incidentally, what made this tribute truly worth having was that he took me for an Englishman, which I partly am.) And the same thought was sounded in different keys by much of the international riffraff that passed through Morocco, Gibraltar, and the Hashish Belt, as well as by the swells we met in Biarritz.

This is not to say that JFK was our first

In 1959, Jack had begun his race for the Democratic presidential nomination. He was one of seven unannounced candidates, most of whom, like Lyndon Johnson, Stuart Symington, and Hubert Humphrey, were better known and infinitely more experienced than he. Here, Jack and Jackie find themselves in a school gymnasium in Washington State, listening to a high-school student's welcome.

FOLLOWING PAGES: Jack Kennedy loved the water. He was a superb swimmer, a fine sailor. Here, during a campaign break in the summer of 1959, Jack and Jackie enjoy themselves immensely, navigating a tiny boat in Hyannis Port, Massachusetts.

13

popular president overseas. Truman and Eisenhower were both immensely popular, but specifically as "friends of Europe" or wherever, while Roosevelt of course was the biggest friend of all. But few Americans had any idea (you had to live there) of the condescension woven into such popularity: condescension for an earnest provincial like Truman, or for a good-hearted bumbler like Eisenhower, who, in their opinion, could neither conduct a battle nor complete a sentence entirely on his own; or even for Roosevelt, the best we could do in the way of an aristocrat but also something of a humbug, an actor out of Mark Twain and at times a truly simpleminded orator talking down to an obviously simple-minded public.

Heaven forfend that we should ever conduct our politics to impress such Europeans—but how much time and trouble it saves when we do! Adlai Stevenson, as I learned at Oxford in 1952, impressed the intellectuals over there mightily—but perhaps for that very reason they were not at all surprised when he lost: Adlai was a species of honorary European anyway and probably much too good for us.

Jack Kennedy, on the other hand, was pure, unconvertible American—and they still liked him. There was, to be sure, an element of Irish luck in this. But his popularity was to some extent also an agreeable sign of changing times, part of a general thaw in the Cold Peace between us and our allies. It seemed that post-war resentment of United States power could not last forever, any more than the power itself could. By courtesy of the Marshall Plan and their own bootstraps, Europeans were starting to catch up with us to the point where they could actually afford to eat in their own restaurants and sleep in their own hotels. So they no longer needed so desperately to look for points of superiority over their liberators.

And there was a change on our side too. By the time I got over there in mid-1961, I found that the omnipresent Mid-American voice seemed to have receded somewhat—those women hollering for "jooo-nior" to come out from behind that shrine, and those men trying to joust with the waiters in Milwaukee French. For their part, even Parisians began to border on the polite. In short, the years of semi-empire had taught both teams a thing or two, and the time was ripe for a Jack Kennedy.

But just because the time is ripe for something doesn't always mean it gets it, and by a dubious eyelash (one of Mayor Daley's, I believe), it almost got Richard Nixon instead, who would have been as exactly wrong for the moment as Kennedy was right. Accustomed as we are, or at least were, to slightly ridiculous politicians over here, we haven't always seen what freaks men like Nixon and Hubert Humphrey (able though they both were) can appear to others. What Kennedy presented to the world

On January 2, 1960, in the caucus room of the U.S. Capitol, Senator Kennedy announces his intention to seek his party's nomination for President of the United States.

was something entirely different and original: an American politician who actually seemed as if he might have done something else for a living.

But more than that, Jack seemed to embody what he himself proposed as a desideratum: that is, a new *kind* of American, one who had to be assessed from scratch, without reference to old images and expectations. This was partly a matter of his unusual sophistication, a gift which our politicians had usually been at some pains to hide if by mischance they had it to begin with, but it was a new *kind* of sophistication too, accessible to everyone (in fact, some of its elements have since surfaced in caricature form in the Yuppie style: but not its essence—i.e., being cool and laid back are not enough).

So perhaps there *was* a new quality in the American air those days. And when Kennedy spoke of a whole "new generation, tempered by war," etc., it was almost possible to believe that there might indeed be more at home like him. Perhaps the recent monster bloodbath—our second, Europe's zillionth—had at last washed away that indelible innocence of ours, and made grown-ups of us for the first time in our history (European version).

Mind you, I am talking so far only of impressions, not necessarily of realities, and not necessarily of *political* realities—although Europe's and the world's impressions of Kennedy would soon enough form a mighty political reality in themselves, with reverberant consequences.

But the subject right now is impressions, and first impressions at that. When President Kennedy first hit the Continent in the spring of 1961, it was almost as if he were picking up a stitch in history. The last American many Europeans had really liked was sitting on top of a tank, smiling down at them, the eternal GI Joe; but now it must have seemed to some as if that good soldier had come back at last after burying himself in gray flannel and blandness for fifteen long years. And it is not enough to put this response down simply to "charisma," that vague word of the period that was always being waved about in his honor, a word practically invented for Kennedy (at least I scarcely remember having ever heard it before, outside of religious circles). Reagan has, I suppose, charisma; but even if his politics were twice as wise as I think they are, and he were twice as young as he is, he would never have rung that particular bell. People *like* Reagan all right, but they don't feel that they have to do anything about it: liking is an end in itself.

What Kennedy conveyed, by contrast, could perhaps best be boiled down to the word "hope." Suddenly, in that spring of 1961, and with

The senator would try to get home as often as possible from his campaign trips, which were piled on top of his Senate duties. Here he is with Jackie and their daughter, Caroline, on the porch of the Kennedys' Hyannis Port home.

General de Gaulle* back in his real saddle—as opposed to his imaginary one—everything seemed possible again. Kennedy's youthfulness, which had been vainly held against him in the election, did not seem to faze the Europeans at all: they had seen enough of our old men. As the Bible says, "Your old men shall dream dreams, your young men shall see visions." And after eight years of dozing along with Ike, perhaps it was time to try a vision or two.

And if anyone looked and sounded as if he saw visions, it was Jack Kennedy in that year of grace. Again, timing was crucial. It had taken Europe this many years to dig itself out from the rubble caused by the last great visionary, and for most of that time the last thing it wanted to see was another one of any description. The swift ouster of the warrior Churchill in Britain and the installation of Konrad "Old Man" Adenauer in Germany indicated what they had in mind for right now: a good, long nap. And even so modest and inevitable a plan as Schuman's European Common Market had to wait its turn until the public got back its wind.

*For over a century, many Frenchmen had waited, wistfully or mockingly, for "a man on a white horse"—i.e., a military savior, and de Gaulle, of course, looked as if he was sitting on a horse even when he wasn't. But the general had been kept waiting on the sidelines in this condition for many years.

And even when it had got it back, more or less, not just any old visionary would have done. What made Kennedy a dreamer to bet on were two qualities his very presence seemed to radiate, one of which could be faked and another which could not, and these were decency and intelligence.

Since then, the decency in particular has come under energetic questioning, and indeed it does not seem to have extended invariably to his dealings with women (although whose does? to paraphrase Bernard Shaw). I have my own thoughts about that, which I'll get to later. But Europeans, and perhaps most other non-Americans, have never equated sexual honor with the political variety. And as for the latter, Kennedy seemed and still seems a great deal cleaner than most—if one excepts for now the grand old American custom of buying elections, or having them bought for you, of which he was sporadically accused (but more on this later). Anyhow, the outside world knew nothing of Cook County, Illinois, voting machines or West Virginia primaries. All it saw, or thought it saw, was a man who would not willfully bring harm to anyone, and who, if he indeed had a vision, would probably have one that could bear the light of day; and, finally, a man whose word—if one allows for the slippery conventions of politics—

JFK leaves for the Senate from his home on N Street in Washington's Georgetown section.

FOLLOWING PAGES: Portland, Oregon. The year is 1959, and Jack, on one of his campaign swings, is met by three supporters, led by Congresswoman Edith Green (center). The others in the picture are Jackie, his aide Dave Powers, and the pilot of his plane. In time this lonely scene became his favorite photograph.

it shining out of the kind of candid, open American face that one would like so much to like if it wasn't so often suffused with an almost criminal ignorance of other people's affairs.

So far, much of what I have written could be read partly as satire on the Europeans of the period, if it weren't for the period itself. Six years of horror, which we could barely imagine from our own safe distance, followed by more years of shortage and second-class status on their own continent (Englishmen could take only £50 to Europe as late as 1961), had not left their judgments altogether clear or kind in the matter of Americans: nobody likes to be poor and indebted at the same time. But alongside the bitterness ran a forlorn wish that Americans could somehow someday be *better* than we were, that we would really *be* the light of the world instead of just bragging about it. And here, as I say, Europeans suddenly saw hope.

My book opens overseas because so many domestic revisionists chipping industriously away at Kennedy's monument (sometimes justly: most monuments start out too big) tend to overlook his international mission in every respect except for specific policies, and the self-evident success or failure thereof. But policies, with their vast baggage of variables, are infinitely controvertible, and their success is seldom self-evident: I'll try to assess some of

could probably be trusted at least a little bit. This at a minimum is what his face, voice, and bearing conveyed to my habitually suspicious hosts of that year: and if it was a trick, it fooled a globeful of people and was once more a significant fact in itself.

As for intelligence, *this* is the one that cannot be faked. One can question, as I sometimes do myself, the uses Kennedy might occasionally put it to, but not the gift itself. And this of course is what truly captivated the Europeans. Decency is all very well in its place, but it flirts dangerously with that old American vice naïveté, and in any event, you wouldn't want to try it around, say, Khrushchev. But with the sacred gift of intelligence, you can go anywhere. And what a double joy to find

The Kennedy family plane, The Caroline, *a DC3, was turned into an office and home in the early days of the campaign. Here, JFK is at work with brother-in-law Steve Smith* (left) *and journalists* (above).

Kennedy's wins and losses, draws and split decisions later. But a presidency is much more than just the sum of its policies. There is also the question of what life *felt* like during those years—and whether that feeling was ultimately worth anything (what might be called the Calvin Coolidge test).

The first thing to be said about the Kennedy feeling was that it was closely linked to action, to getting things "moving again," and not only in the United States, but in what we optimistically call the free world as well. The *intelligent* good will generated by Kennedy had an obvious ripple effect, from leaders like de Gaulle and Harold Macmillan on down to street level and below, and thus other nations' policies may have been affected by it, besides our own. Kennedy's sense of possibility had an almost contagious quality to it—you could catch it even in Franco's Spain—and it is my own unsubstantiated bet that in many odd corners of the globe, from Africa to South America, even to motionless India itself, things began to stir in their sleep, not always directly because of Kennedy but as part of a long chain reaction to his legendary vitality. And if this isn't greatness, it might as well be.

All right, concedes an indulgent revisionist of my own invention, maybe he did perform some of these putative miracles on the strength of a pleasant manner and a radiant wife (whom,

Through much of the early campaign, Jackie shared the rigors of the road; the loneliness of that effort becomes very apparent here.

incidentally, you seem to have forgotten completely), but you can't give *him* credit for that. We live in star-struck times, and the Kennedys were stars, and everyone had a swell time at the party.

There obviously is some truth in that—a politician must function within the superstitions of his times, and although 1961 was a far cry from 1988 (we didn't have either an actor-president or *People* magazine back then), yes, the Kennedys did indeed help introduce the Star System to American politics. They could hardly have helped it, but to use the word in another sense, perhaps they didn't have to help it quite as much as they did. However, as I shall have more than one occasion to point out, a politician should not be confused with his relatives. Jackie did indeed put a smile, like unto her own, on the rest of the world, for a season. But Jackie did not give anyone fresh hope in nuclear sanity or rational treaties rationally arrived at, or offer any abiding relief to the literally splitting headaches left over from World War II. That was all Jack: and if it was only hope that he finally had the time, or perhaps the capacity, to give us, it was also more than charm that gave it.

Toward the shank of our exile in June 1961, a vintage example occurred of Kennedy at once using his charm and going well beyond it. The Russians had just run the Berlin Wall up, apparently overnight, and Kennedy, who might

The campaigning couple take the pledge of allegiance at yet another high school.

INTERNATIONAL

or might not have been able to do something about this earlier, now decided to make the best of a bad job by addressing a speech more or less to the wall itself.

Although his famous *"Ich bin ein Berliner"* declaration did not exactly bring the wall tumbling down (he wasn't Joshua), there was no doubt, by the time he had finished, that the wall seemed to be facing squarely in the other direction. "Democracy may not be perfect," he said, "but we have never had to put a wall up to keep our people in, to prevent them from leaving us." And it wasn't just his words. By planting himself with such high-spirited defiance in the very shadow of the wall, he showed that the masonry represented no actual power, that it was just a wall. Beyond that, if the Russians wanted to build a prison around their own people, so be it: such a prison only served to remind people on the outside of how free they were.

"Ich bin ein Berliner." The Russians had in fact presented Kennedy with a golden opportunity to assert America's solidarity with Western Europe in a setting that smacked of actual danger, at the site of our most inflamed pressure point. Mind you, such assertions were ten a penny in those days, and usually worth about as much: nobody listened anymore. But they listened that day. I have since learned that the word *"Berliner"* doubles as the brand name of a certain type of doughnut, which might have tickled the crowd's attention. But

if the Germans found it funny, they were cheering too loudly to laugh. And even in the English cricket ground where I chanced to be at the time, a round of hearty, uncricketlike applause went up when the news seeped in.

It was absolutely the best Kennedy could have done that day. But, pipes our revisionist, wasn't it mostly a public-relations victory anyway? Indeed it was—at a time when we needed one badly. But yes, the wall remained in the same place, where it didn't *really* suit us: nothing tangible had changed. If, however, one considers the incident in the total context of transatlantic unity as envisaged by Kennedy, such victories could be priceless, and an absolute prerequisite for more substantial ones.

So: do we finally just credit Kennedy for being extremely good at being himself? Well, if the invariably apt word, the right response, and what Scott Fitzgerald once called "an unbroken series of perfect gestures" (well, almost unbroken) can really be arrived at without effort, then Kennedy was truly among the blessed and quite beyond praise—especially if he could pull it off while allegedly concealing intense, almost constant back pain.

However, since I am ending this chapter in an English cricket ground, a slightly more English alternative strikes me. Jack had of course logged some youthful time in that country, absorbing who knows what in matters of style. But we do know that he much admired Lord Melbourne, the debonair prime minister who

In West Virginia, JFK climbs on a tractor to address a group of grade-schoolers.

31

once upon a time undertook to play Henry Higgins to the crude German princess Victoria, turning her eventually into a passable queen; and we also know that the Melbournes of this world strove, and still strive, at all times to live up to the Balliol College ideal of "effortless superiority." In other words, one must never appear to try too hard; and of course it goes without saying that one must *never*, unlike the unfortunate Mr. Nixon, appear to sweat.

I have referred to Kennedy earlier as a pure American, but almost by definition this often includes bits and pieces of other nationalities. And it could be that in the end what really assured certain Europeans—those at least with long memories—about our young president was that he reminded them ever so slightly of one of those cool nineteenth-century English politicians who had helped so much to keep Europe out of truly major wars for almost a century, between 1815 and 1914.

Who knows? Perhaps Europe's good luck had returned at last.

Joseph P. Kennedy, a former ambassador to the Court of St. James and a strong, ambitious, and powerful figure, was anxious to formulate campaign strategy and philosophy. Yet Jack kept him in the background and succeeded in shedding the conservative, isolationist image his father represented.

T W O

The View from Home

My wife and I returned to the U.S. that fall to find the party in full swing. But before plunging into that, I'd like to back-track just one year to consider how it all, incredibly, began.

"Who d'you like in the election?" asked a wise old Irish friend of mine in the fall of 1960.

"Jack Kennedy," I said, "against my better judgment."

"Me too," he said with that gloomy relish peculiar to his tribe.

So what *was* this better judgment that we were both so agreed about, and why did we both so grandly decide to overlook it for now? The

On August 1, 1943, at 2:30 A.M., PT boat 109, commanded by Lieutenant (j.g.) John F. Kennedy, was sliced in half and sunk by a Japanese destroyer. Kennedy, already suffering from a bad back, was slammed to the floor, which severely injured his spine. In spite of his injury, Kennedy located twelve survivors. Next morning, with Kennedy firmly grasping his wounded engineer's life belt between his teeth, the two swam to safety at a nearby island. Ever since then, the future president suffered from severe back pain, and the rocking chair became an essential comfort to him.

case against Jack in 1960 may prove as good a way to introduce him as any: and it too would be a very Irish way of proceeding.

I'm sure, to begin with, that my friend's better judgment was much better than mine—in fact some of mine could hardly be called judgment at all, but rather whim, hunch, and prejudice, the usual voter's tool kit. But such as it was, my "better judgment" may help to convey how warily many people still felt about embracing Jack just three short years before he became a national martyr and saint.

At that early stage most of what the general public knew about Jack it got from the gossip columns, which gravely informed us that he was dashing, glamorous, and a new face—a hundred different ways of saying "lightweight," to my jaundiced mind. But in those days only a handful of fanatics knew what actually went on in the Congress, and candidates had not yet hit upon the device of taking two years off from work to parade themselves around the country becoming known. So the average working senator had about the name recognition of a bit player in the movies: hence the extreme difficulty (and rarity) of men who have made the leap directly from the Hill to the Big House.

We did know even then that Jack had a reputation for being a somewhat lazy senator* and a somewhat more energetic ladies' man: and I sometimes wondered why the Republicans didn't make more use of the latter in the subterranean branch of their campaign against him. (I concluded on this that the GOP might have sensed that public feelings are not all that clear or predictably edifying in respect to virile leaders so long as the virility is mostly based on rumor—getting caught brings us to our senses.) We also knew that Jack was a war hero, but Capitol Hill was crawling with those, real and imaginary, in the forties, and we hadn't yet sorted out the mountebanks;† and offsetting the war record was the rather obvious fact that he had to be a rather young man to have acquired it, so there was much chitchat about what constituted "too young" for the presidency. World War II had obliged us to revise our notion about what was "too young" to lead troops into combat, so our minds were still more open on such matters than in the past.

*This was before we knew about Jack's murderous back troubles, brought on by his war injuries, which enforced a certain amount of absenteeism.

†It took a while to sift through the sheer braggadocio of their campaign literature to realize how few pols actually saw any action at all. Kennedy's feat of saving three members of his PT crew from drowning in the Pacific gains even more stature if you consider how hard it is to save *one* man in quite peaceful waters.

Early in the campaign, it was hard for Kennedy to find anyone willing to listen to his message "to get the country going again." Here, on a Sunday morning after Mass, at a local coffee shop across the street from the Let 'Er Buck motel, where they had spent the night, Jack, Jackie, and brother-in-law Steve Smith sit, ignored by the locals, having breakfast. Six months later, all that would change, and both Jack and Jackie would be swamped by people eager to touch them.

Still, Jack would be our first president born not only in this century but in the second decade of this century: a mere puppy indeed.

Age was certainly no factor in my set, which had wondered for some time why presidents always had to be so ancient, and why one had to wait so long for everything worth having in life. But an argument I had one night with an apoplectic businessman instructed me sharply that older voters might feel a bit different about this (I had said that forty-two was plenty old enough to run a big company and he had said—naturally—"Just wait till you're older, sonny"), and I was afraid that Jack might be stuck with the youth vote (which still began at twenty-one) and not much else.

What really bothered me about Jack, though, went more like this: if, as rumor had it, the House rather bored him and the Senate bored him too, why on earth did he want to be president? Was it just for the greater glory of it? Or was it (and this wasn't as crazy as it sounds) mainly to please his father? One of the odd scraps of folklore that had drifted out of World War II was the saga of how Joseph P. Kennedy, the buccaneer business giant, had more or less wished the presidency on his oldest son, Joseph, Jr., someday, and of how afterward, when Joe was killed in action, the old man had simply reached down for another son, Jack, and laid the wish on him, as if any member of the family would do so long as it was *his* family.

Most Americans, presumably, had mixed feelings about having their leader chosen for them in precisely this way, and I believe that Father Joe's famous blessing became in many ways a curse, clouding everything Jack accomplished on his own in the early going. Even his Pulitzer Prize (for *Profiles in Courage*) and the publicity for his wartime exploits were scrutinized—couldn't his old man buy *everything*? And when Jack won smashing victories in every Massachusetts election he entered, his whole family had seemed to blanket the state, as if they were all running for office in a body. (And didn't old Joe own the territory anyway?) It is hard for a rich kid to get credit for anything.

As for Jack himself, he seemed all too willing to go along with the scenario, and from a certain perspective his whole career seemed shaped for the presidency, as if no other job in the world was worthy of him. As a congressman and senator, he made wonderful presidential speeches (most notably, a rousing plea for Algerian independence, which may in a farfetched way be considered his first link to General de Gaulle), but made no attempt whatever to be a great parliamentarian or floor-fighter, presumably because being one can be a dangerous game for future presidents to play

Here in Coos Bay, Oregon, a lonely Kennedy discusses the race with a local supporter.

FOLLOWING PAGES: *In a union hall in Coos Bay, Oregon, Jackie joins the longshoremen audience as the candidate addresses a glum, sparsely attended, nearly hostile union meeting.*

In West Virginia, Kennedy toured the rural regions. Although his name was not a household word, recognition was beginning to take hold.

and Jack was playing it safe all the way. Thus his votes were consistently *not* the kind that later come back and haunt you, and he left his name on no controversial legislation. So there were no jagged political edges on the missile as it took off.

But, of course, if you subtract Joe Kennedy and his famous dream from this picture, all this takes on a slightly different cast. Jack actually drifted into politics in 1946 in a somewhat despondent state, not because he was driven to it but because he couldn't find anything else he liked better. And he found when he got there that, whatever the name might stand for in parts of Boston, the Kennedys definitely did *not* own Massachusetts in those

days, let alone the United States. In fact, when Jack defeated Henry Cabot Lodge for the Senate in 1952, a year when Dwight Eisenhower was mowing down Adlai Stevenson in the same state, it was considered a stunning upset—so much so that the political pros quickly began to consider him for the vice presidency in 1956. This went way beyond anything the Kennedy name or money could do (you didn't outspend a Lodge easily). Jack was simply a great candidate in his own right, whatever else he might be, and if the Kennedys later *seemed* to own the state it was more his doing than anyone else's.

Similarly, if we forget the king-making blarney for a moment, it seems possible that young congressman Jack may have figured out on his own and at an early stage that his talents were presidential and not collegial, in which case his cautious behavior in the Senate makes perfectly good sense. Barry Goldwater and George McGovern would later demonstrate exactly how far a conservative record and a liberal one, respectively, will get you on the national stage. Conversely, Gary Hart and others would later show for all time the wisdom of simply lighting out from that House of Pitfalls, the Senate, altogether and becoming a pure candidate. As such, Gary could go Jack even one better by giving *nothing* but speeches and never voting at all, becoming almost as ethereal as a state governor, that most ideal of candidates (outside of a famous general). So it might be fair to consider Jack a transitional figure between the old breed of candidate and the later models; in which role let's just say he made some remarkable speeches, missed remarkably few roll calls for a man whose health was then at its screaming worst, and cast some respectable votes: but most of all, he went to school to politics. And, more than most, he went abroad—also to politics: because for such a temperament, the whole world becomes a political university.

During those working or idling years, it was at last possible to contemplate Jack on his own, feeling his own way toward statesmanship, and forget for minutes on end that he even had a family. But the very word "election" seemed to act on the clan like a dinner bell, and out they all came pouring in 1960. And there seemed to be so many of them—and not simply their multitudinous selves but hosts of honorary Kennedys, commissioned on the battlefield whenever the Kennedys needed another Kennedy.

Government by Family: it was a daunting thought, especially government by this one. Minus Jack, they presented a formidable surface of apparent strength as they swarmed over the campaign like storm troopers. So it's worth taking time out for a brief whiff of them.

The Kennedys were fabulous creatures long before Jack came along. In fact they may have been the best-known family to spawn a president since the Adamses hit their stride: but they were not known for particularly presidential things. Unlike the Roosevelts of Hyde Park and Oyster Bay, they did not exude quiet dignity, or anything approaching it. Perched someplace between Boston street politics and café society, their trademark was competitiveness and more competitiveness. Through the Catholic underground I had long since heard reports of the pugnacious energy of Jack's immediate siblings: I was told, for instance, that it was as much as your life was worth to step onto the hockey field with one of his sisters, while Bobby in his pre-converted state carried himself, in public at least, like the hit man in a prep-school gang.

The family motto seemed to be "Us against the world," an attitude which quickly bred an equal and opposite reaction toward them on the world's part. But what had the world ever done to them to deserve this? Was there some historic insult to be avenged? Perhaps. Although I gather that tales of the Kennedys' overt rejection by WASP society have been

somewhat exaggerated, rejection doesn't have to be overt and there doesn't have to be much of it. I do recall overhearing some Philadelphia dowagers refer to the Kennedys as out-and-out guttersnipes, and a horrible example of what Society was coming to. And even the top Irish families, who had made their fortunes barely five minutes earlier, tended to look down on the Kennedys too, ranking them almost as low as the Kellys of Philadelphia (who later, of course, gave us Princess Grace).

Someone once called John O'Hara "the master of the fancied slight," and Irish-Americans were undoubtedly a touchy lot during the transition years from bog to lace curtain to Oval Office. But where most of them seemed content to climb the social ladder in clusters and by the old rules, the Kennedys climbed alone.

Consider the following contrast. When the first wave of top Irish families struck out socially in Newport, they simply descended on Southampton and swarmed over the country club there instead, eventually becoming as stuffy and colorless as the next fat cat. But the Kennedys didn't seem to think that that kind of ladder was even worth climbing, let alone being snubbed over. Their own family compounds, especially Hyannis Port, were usually quite enough country club for them. And in these inbred garrisons they were not only free to maintain their own swashbuckling style, which

was quite unlike that of any rich people I have ever met, but to hone their competitive edge on each other between bouts with the world. There, too, the Founding Father, Joseph P. Kennedy, could groom his boys to make an end run around Society, and someday wind up in front of it as nothing less than presidents.

Since then, Hyannis Port has been revealed and overrevealed as a jolly, playful sort of place, where, outside of having to play touch football on demand and being randomly shoved into swimming pools, they treated you okay. But at the time I, at least, pictured something a little harsher: some sort of youth camp, perhaps, where "strength through joy" was practiced around the clock, the competition never let up, and the whole family went to bed chanting "Don't get mad, get even." And I wasn't sure I wanted a president raised in such a peculiar place.

Jack Kennedy's startling wit would soon blow these gloomy fantasies away, or at least down to size, and in their place Jack would lend the whole family a share of his own special grace. And it is here that we might start separating Jack gently from his kin. For instance, neither of his brothers had ever shown any particular sign either of ease or charm; but insofar as their voices and faces began to remind one of Jack's, they did seem sort of charming at that. They even seemed sort of witty, which is a truly amazing feat of transference. I may be

TOP AND BOTTOM: *The search for votes and hands to shake was difficult in the early days of the West Virginia primary. Few voters cared. In retrospect, the poignancy of this seemingly hopeless task, only eight months before Inauguration Day, is shattering.*

FOLLOWING PAGES: *The candidate campaigning late at night in Wilmette, Illinois.*

doing someone an injustice here, but I have never to this day actually heard any other Kennedy say anything funny that didn't sound rehearsed—but suddenly that was quite good enough for us. If it sounded like Jack, it *must* be funny.*

And it wasn't just the Kennedy sound: it was also the way he talked about the other Kennedys. When, for instance, Jack announced that he was appointing Bobby Attorney General so that his brother could get a little legal experience before going into practice, or when he invented that telegram from his father saying "I promised to buy you an election, but I'm damned if I'm going to pay for a landslide," he was implicating his family in the fun: it seemed that somehow Bobby and old Joseph P. were taking part in those jokes too, and must be funny people in their own right.

This sharing of his own gift of humor with his not outstandingly humorous relatives did wonders to take the curse off the famous Kennedy ruthlessness in 1960: where before, the clan might well have been perceived as a pack

*In his last years (though he was still much too young to be having last years) Bobby suddenly began making some pretty good jokes himself, though in a slightly startled voice, as if he had inherited even that along with his political goals from his brother. In fact, I'm told that Bobby had always had his droll moments in private, but they must have been very private indeed.

By the time of the Wisconsin and West Virginia primaries, the Kennedy plane, The Caroline, *visited twelve states in one five-week period, some of these several times. Given this hectic schedule, the plane became an oasis of calm, a place to reflect and take stock. Here, flying over Nevada on his way to California, Kennedy smokes one of his favorite stogies.*

of hard-eyed, ambitious hustlers, they now seemed merely coltish and high-spirited. It would be *fun* to award them with a president.

Observe further the political art of the above jokes: Jack was accusing himself outright of nepotism and his father of doing exactly that which the nation feared most, and making it all sound like a wonderful prank. (In fact, Bobby would go on amply to justify himself as Attorney General, and Poppa Joe, hard as he undoubtedly tried, no more bought the election for Jack than the perennially richer Republican coffers bought it for Nixon. But for Jack to forestall objections on both incendiary fronts before they got started and to score points at the same time—that took some kind of political genius.)

Jack's wit, however, had other fish to fry besides sprucing up the family legend; it also, to my mind, served to detach him a measure or two from same. By the very act of seeming amused by his relatives, he removed himself from them slightly. Even vis-à-vis his all-powerful father, Jack's posture seemed lofty: as if to say, I make the jokes around here, you just take part in them.

It was essentially a humor of detachment anyway, and I guessed then, and believe firmly today, that Jack began using it early to gain breathing and thinking room in the Kennedy compound. Reports suggest that his older brother, Joe, Jr., bullied him a bit, and his father of course must have seemed intellectually suffocating whether he wanted to or not (I gather he did not, but ran the never-ending discussion groups on egalitarian lines: yet both Bobby and Teddy grew up to wear slightly apprehensive expressions, perhaps from trying to think too fast when they were young). It took courage to grow up in that family, and it must have taken some willpower to resist the old man's ideas, and Jack's wit was probably used in the service of both: possibly to disarm Joe, Jr., and undoubtedly to see around and behind his father's opinions.

If Jack was the family wit, he was also, without contest, the family intellectual. In group photos of the others you will see many qualities, but not that one. The basic Kennedy mind, stripped to essentials, was and presumably is a can-do mind, and the family debates must have skipped as quickly as possible to "Does it work?" and (perhaps in honor of sainted Mother Rose) "Is it right?" Bobby would later show as Attorney General how surprisingly far you can go on these two questions alone: and

TOP: Smoke-filled rooms, city bosses, and old-fashioned "pols" are now a thing of the past. But in the campaign of 1960, they still played a large role. Here, Kennedy participates in a hasty strategy conference at a room in the Chicago airport before flying on to Wisconsin.

BOTTOM: Jackie signing autographs for students at a California high school.

the family bull sessions had trained him to get there like a whippet. Since this in turn would play a part in Bobby's famous decisiveness, which would someday prove such a godsend to brother Jack, it is worth noting that more than one kind of mind was honed to maximum sharpness by Joseph P.'s Socratic methods. (The old man, for all his quirks, was one hell of a teacher, in his little college for presidents.)

But "intellectual" is something else altogether. Intellect is the gift that, so to speak, springs you from the inlets of your own questions, where most of us paddle vigorously in circles, into the sea of a million questions. As soon as Father Joe spotted this quality in Jack, he made one of his most curious and admirable moves: he sent the boy straight into the enemy camp, to the London School of Economics and to Harold Laski—the very bastion and bastion-keeper of radical socialist thought. "No son of mine could ever be a blankety-blank liberal," Joe would later assure Harry Luce in 1960; but he must have had his doubts when he placed Jack's young head in the Bear's mouth back in 1935. The perhapses are endless on this one, but one imagines that a son like Jack must have been a new adventure and Joe was an adventurer; also that Joe, Sr., also wanted to keep handsome Jack serious, which meant challenged; and, finally, that he could always console himself with Joe, Jr., as his "next president of the United States of America." (Joe, Jr., incidentally, had also been exposed to Laski, with perfect safety: compared with Jack, Joe was no gamble at all.)

Whatever Jack may or may not have learned from Laski, he seems to have learned much more from his attendant travels, which included a sweep of Europe and the Middle East. His punctilious reports home from the "trouble spots" (and everywhere was a trouble spot in 1939) reveal the true nature of his intellectual gift, which consisted essentially of compendious and dead-accurate observation of actual people, places, and events, followed by remarkably sage judgment on all. This gift would grow enormously with the years, and he would make precious few mistakes with either countries or politicians he had met personally. As Justice William Douglas would later put it (and I paraphrase), once Jack had spent an hour with, say, Jawaharlal Nehru of India, he knew exactly what to expect of him and was never surprised (which only makes one wish that he had been present at Versailles and Yalta. In fact, it's hard to think of any other president since the Founders who could judge foreigners at all).

"I want all my kids to grow up and spit in my eye," said the curious Joseph P., and insofar as it was in him to do so, he instilled enough character in most of them to perform that deceptively difficult task many times over. But Jack alone had, so to speak, the intellectual ammunition for it as well. And although he respected his father too much to do the actual spitting, and perhaps in some subterranean sense was daunted by him too, Jack did once say casually that if he ever decided to run for commissar he was certain that his father would be out there the next day handing out leaflets for him. This jolts the mind for a moment. Suppose, just suppose, that one turns

Jack Kennedy campaigning at Mills College in Oakland, California.

the picture upside down for a flash—could it possibly be that old Joe, far from trying to stage-manage his brilliant son, was happy almost from the beginning simply to be scurrying about in his service, doing whatever he could to help the next King of the Kennedys? Stranger things have happened in Irish families.

As noted, the Europeans had respected Jack's intellect on sight for what it was.* Americans

---

*I am making no claims here for genius, but only for a kind of mind rare in politics, that of a true, if still-untested, philosopher king.

liked it too, but we call it something else over here. (Americans have their own good and bad reasons for distrusting the word.) But it was absolutely crucial to his victory in 1960. In his brief oral history of the Kennedys, Justice Douglas also noted that young Jack never *seemed* like a scholar, and to the public he never would. Instead, he displayed merely the essence of intellect, the quick grasp of subjects, the imagination and gift for conjecture, and the plentiful time left over for wit. While the world was still puzzling over the secret of

---

FOLLOWING PAGES: The smiling but relatively ignored candidate in Ona, West Virginia.

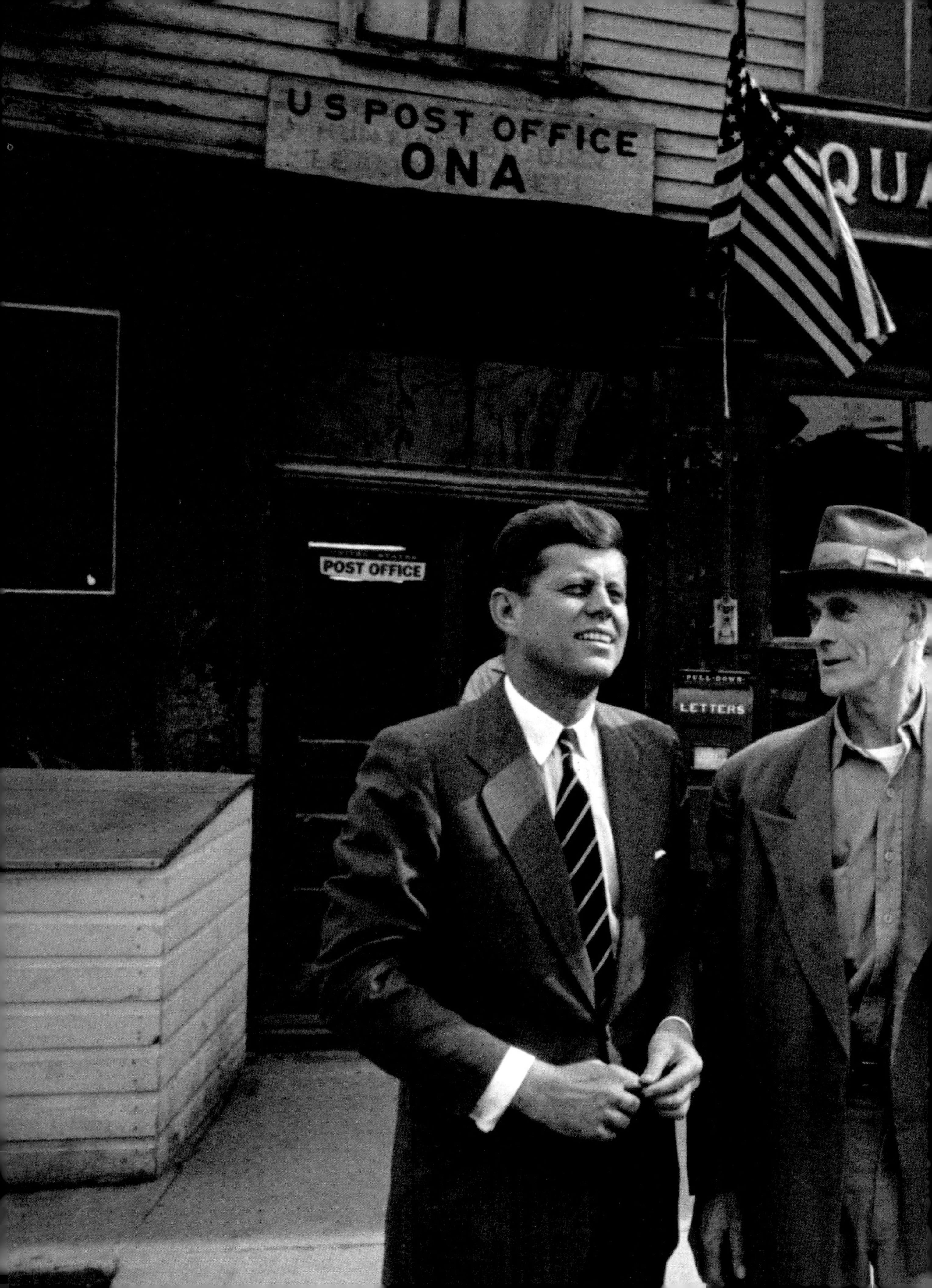
US POST OFFICE
ONA
POST OFFICE
LETTERS
QUA

Jack's high and low appeal (charisma gets you the one kind but not both), I preferred to think of him in terms of the one teacher in school whom you actually liked, the one who didn't really seem like a teacher at all. Even in his off-the-cuff speeches and press conferences, I felt that this unteacher-teacher was always present, poking his head through the rhetoric, ready to teach and learn. And although Jack may not usually be listed among our Educational Presidents, I can't think offhand of any who tried harder to explain things and less to obfuscate them. But, to repeat dolefully, we didn't know any of this in 1960.

It is sobering to realize how many books we might have been spared, or deprived of, as you see fit, concerning the Kennedy legend if Jack had gone down with his PT boat in the Pacific, and if his older brother had completed all his missions unscathed.

Suppose for instance that Joe, Jr., had indeed survived the war to run for president at his father's bidding. Well, we would at least have seen a *real* Kennedy out there, the undiluted, un-Laskied thing. Joe had already shown ample signs of being his father's son, virtually a carbon copy, politically speaking; and if I add that he strikes me as a bit of a lout, and that nothing I've read about him indicates anything like the stature to break the religious barrier to the presidency, it is only to show how close the Kennedy legend came

to being a much more modest affair than it is—although it is to *that* legend that some historians seem to be consigning Jack when they equate him with his family.

If Joe had tried and failed, it would still have been bad news for the legend, because there is no logical reason to suppose that either Bobby or Teddy, flying solo, could have come within a mile of the presidency. Only by clinging to the memory of Jack's coattails could they have gotten as close as they did. Bobby, who might have made a genuinely great president, was a lackluster candidate, even with Jack's example to go by, and many people just never took to him even later, when he was Jack's standard bearer; while Teddy, to keep this polite, would have come much too late. So the only Kennedy capable of fulfilling his father's dream was the Kennedy least like his father: which figures, because his father was widely considered one of the most unelectable men in America.

In fact, the whole clan needed something added to it before it could play outside of Boston. Bobby would later prove to have tremendous administrative gifts, and would almost become that side of Jack's brain, and Teddy had a few gifts too (the family voted him "best politician," which I take to be a fond consolation prize), they might both have made interesting chapters in a history of Boston politics.

But Jack's ascendancy transported them all to a higher plane where—and here the legend

JFK with his close aide Ted Sorensen at the 1960 Democratic convention in Los Angeles prior to his nomination.

is germane—he knew exactly how to use* them, and they exactly how to make themselves useful. Teddy was to become a beachhead for Jack in Congress, Bobby would become merely indispensable, and Father Joe would get out of town and lie low while his old contacts delivered their old votes. Jackie, of course, would be herself. Such a family is a handy thing to have around, but the only sinister thing about them, once we got to know them

*The word "use" has a special, technical meaning in politics. Any politician who can will certainly "use" his wife and children, and possibly even his dog and his wife's coat. If we leave out the dog and the coat, the other usages are not only expected, but virtually insisted on by the voting public—with the tacit understanding that the wife and family are using him too. By these standards, Jack Kennedy's exploitation of family was remarkably sensitive and delicate, and everybody gained a little something out of it.

better, seemed to be their uncanny willingness to work together. Brothers and sisters just aren't supposed to *be* like that.

In terms of politics, pure and simple, Bobby and Teddy had already left their father's shadow by 1960 and entered Jack's for life, and old Joseph P.'s conservative adventurism would no longer be the family heritage. It would be Jack's family now, not Joe's. But in 1960 we could not *see* all this delicate in-house reshuffling. The rest of the relatives would soon enough be transformed by Jack's wand, but it remained almost impossible to believe that Joseph P. Kennedy would be able to keep his hands to himself once he had a real live president in the family. And Joseph P. was definitely not what we wanted in Washington, whether behind the scenes or right on stage.

The trouble with accumulations of money and power such as Kennedy's is that it's hard to tell when the original volcano has gone out. So long as the Founding Father had his money, and his breath, he had his power. And his whole life had been an exercise in how to use it. Could he now give it up, just like that? Joseph P.'s flamboyant career has been rehashed often enough to deserve its rest by now: but in all his gaudy phases—as short-term movie mogul, putative rumrunner, Wall Street wizard, and ambassador to Great Britain (the list is wildly abbreviated)—one word always described him precisely and that one is "willful": he did exactly what he wanted.

The ambassadorship provided perhaps the most spectacular public example of this quality and one that would haunt the family image for years to come. In 1940 our affairs with the

British were about as delicate as affairs can get. American anti-war sentiment was still widespread and virulent enough for FDR to have campaigned that very summer on a promise to keep our boys out of it altogether; but now actual German bombs had begun to fall on London, and the slogan "It can't happen here" was gradually giving way to its opposite, while another phrase was moving stealthily into the language, to wit, "All aid short of war." In the circumstances, all that Roosevelt could reasonably do now was make comradely noises to the British, encouraging them to hold out, while waiting for the nightly broadcasts of Edward R. Murrow and others to hammer home, like the blitz itself, the ravening, insatiable lunacy of Hitler for all Americans to see.

But if Joe Kennedy had heard of such a deeply marred policy, he showed no sign of it, and, besides, delicacy wasn't his strong suit, or one of his suits at all. So after examining the situation like a balance sheet, he briskly pronounced, without consulting Washington, that British aid should be dropped altogether like a bad account. England couldn't possibly win, and we were only wasting good American money trying to save it.

The cold-hearted arrogance of such advice, delivered in such a place by a mere ambassador (although Joe was never a "mere" anything), colored the Kennedy memory long after the particular circumstances were forgotten by the average citizen. If Jack was *anything* like his father, that's all we needed to know. Although in real life the man himself had been hauled back to Washington in semi-disgrace

and came out of the affair anything but a winner, the legend was fixed: Joe Kennedy simply did what he liked and got what he wanted, and to hell with the rest of the world.

And we knew what he wanted now—a royal succession in his very own country, issuing straight from him (as I say, any son would do). And we knew or thought we knew how he planned to go about getting it. It was common knowledge (the old man was not shy about his power) that he already had a world-class collection of city bosses sewn into his pocket, lovingly gathered from sea to shining sea— from Charlie Buckley in the Bronx, through Dick Daley in Chicago, to Jesse Unruh in Los Angeles: and such collections tend to multiply almost on their own. As for the primary states: what self-respecting millionaire could not afford to buy West Virginia, at least? There were fewer obligatory primaries in those days, and the Kennedys packed enough sheer manpower, or family power, to blitzkrieg what there were of them without even dipping into capital. Pictures of Hubert Humphrey forlornly clanging his suitcase against his leg as he raced for some commercial airline were contrasted with the ever-ready Kennedy jet, earning Hubert *sympathy*, the last thing a world leader needs. But if Jack thought that life isn't fair, you can imagine what Hubert thought as he puffed over the tarmac.

This, roughly speaking, was the better judgment that my old friend and I were deciding not to use: even Sir Galahad would have seemed tainted after an election engineered by Joseph P. And against all this—what? Only Jack Kennedy himself, as we got to know him that year.

My own experience was about average: the convention, the debates of course, the jolly jousts with the press—and then one sunny day I heard that he was about to appear in Union Square, and I skipped on down to step into the aura for a moment or two: and felt not so much knocked out by it as, well, "cheered up" sounds flat, but something like that. This, as reflected off the faces around me, was suddenly the sunniest day in the history of the world, and it was going to be this way from now on. *That* was the Kennedy effect, as I experienced it.

I've stepped into a great many auras before and since, but never into anything quite like this. More prosaically: Jack seemed bigger and healthier (rumors of Addison's disease had been spread by the LBJ camp, but fortunately we didn't know what it looked like) than I'd expected—in fact, I thought to myself, *Aha, I've got it. Irish monsignor* (all Irish men look like priests if you've known enough of both). He also looked, as advertised, radiant with vitality, confidence, and honest-to-God humor—not the canned kind that candidates drag around wearily from city to city, but a view of life which probably never left him. His whole face would light up with a kind of incredulous merriment as a pleasantry struck him, and there was never any doubt where the jokes came from. He never had to steal one from anybody.

But jokes or no jokes, there was absolutely nothing of the backroom about him. Although he *did* like cigars, God bless him, you couldn't picture him spending five happy minutes in the company of his father's dingy friends and cat's-paws.* And it occurred to me then and later that perhaps Joseph P. had been encumbering his son with the wrong kind of help.

It wasn't yet widely apparent, as it soon would be, that Joseph P.'s backroom boys were beginning to lose the power to make or break *anybody*: they could still help you partway to a party nomination, if the weather was right, but not one inch further. It was already particularly clear in Jack's case that if he were to win a national election—which is too big to fix anyway—he would have to get there by way of an entirely different segment of the populace: younger, but not necessarily; better educated would help; idealistic—in short, the Adlai Stevenson remnant revivified, plus something else, something as yet undefined.

It was a will-o'-the-wisp congregation, which Kennedy just had to take on faith for now, or else call into creation himself. He was further handicapped by the universal understanding that no successful candidate can ever actually say what he intends to do without grave risk

*On this I was wrong. Ben Bradlee assured me that there was always a touch of the Mick about Gentleman Jack, and he quite enjoyed some of the more salty old-timers. But his politics could never be theirs.

Kennedy addressing a skeptical group of labor leaders during the convention.

of shooting himself in the toe.* So—perhaps he could devise some kind of sign language or code to indicate the *kind* of thing he wanted, and the kind of following who would like it.

Since then, I've known a great many members of that generation—to some extent, I suppose, I'm one myself—and I think they might agree that something every bit as intangible as that did indeed happen. They didn't know what they'd been waiting for—and to some degree still didn't after enigmatic encounters like my own in Union Square. (For what it's worth, Jack didn't say anything that day that we hadn't heard a hundred times before.) Like every successful candidate for president—preeminently FDR in 1932—he seemed to be asking the nation either for a blank check, or a full one that he probably wouldn't be able to honor. All Kennedy actually offered was a New Frontier, which could mean whatever you liked. But what his manner suggested was something more like a young officer poised on top of a trench saying, "Follow me, boys, and we'll think of something." Anyway, follow we did.

For this to work on a national scale was another matter: no living person, not even a Kennedy, could meet enough voters in person to mesmerize them one by one; and on TV,

*Viz., Adlai on nuclear testing and strontium 90, Mondale on taxation, McGovern on inherited income, among other things, and Goldwater on everything. If Nixon had announced in advance that he was going to devalue the dollar, invade Cambodia, and visit China, he might also have been spared the embarrassment of winning in '68 and '72. Instead, he merely said that he had "a secret plan to end the war," which may have been the only secret plan he *didn't* have at the time.

Bobby Kennedy, campaign manager and strategist for his brother, in a huddle with Pennsylvania delegates at the convention.

Bobby in his headquarters at the Biltmore Hotel in Los Angeles during the convention.

Jack's image, like most people's, tended to flatten out slightly. He came across as a very pleasant, fresh-faced young man, with a slight, on-the-verge-of-stammering shyness which some consider the hallmark of the gentleman (the Fred Astaire proposition). In fact, Jack might even be taken for somebody's dutiful son, the one thing he emphatically didn't need to be taken for. What did *not* come across through the tube was the virile authority he conveyed in person, and for that he needed a

TV partner, a stooge, if you will, to provide a contrast. And who should be so kind as to volunteer for this thankless part but good old Richard Nixon himself.

Either out of unwonted generosity or hubristic pride in his own debating ability, Nixon consented to not one but three visibility-rich debates with his less-known opponent. Kennedy could hardly have asked for anything more. Nixon had not yet fathomed that TV debating has little or no connection with the real thing. The enduring success of talk shows is based on the discovery that TV works best by letting personalities offset and enlarge one another, and to hell with content. One man speaking alone, be he Billy Graham or even Ronald Reagan, becomes twice the personality if he's suddenly placed next to a Johnny Carson or a Walter Mondale: and presidential campaigns are preeminently measurements for size.

They are also tests of the better poker player, the guy you'd put your bankroll on if you had nothing else to go on but appearances. Truman vs. Dewey, Eisenhower vs. Stevenson, Roosevelt vs. the field: there can be very few if any exceptions to this principle.

But there is a further catch to this. The public's idea of what a good poker player looks like does not necessarily jibe with reality. Off camera, Nixon had played the game itself very well indeed, according to his own accounts, and he would later play its real-life counterpart, diplomacy, with considerable skill. But on camera, he couldn't have bluffed his maiden aunt. Steve McQueen could probably have beaten him just by standing there: but, failing

Steve, Jack would do nicely. And the difference was not just a matter of Nixon's weird-looking makeup. As I've written elsewhere, the two of them could have switched makeup completely without affecting the result in the least.

Because what showed through all the pancake and shadows was, to this naked eye at least, Nixon's whole sense of inferiority to the eastern establishment, which at other times could express itself in snarling resentment but now surfaced as something closer to deference. (If so, it was quite a triumph for the "upstart" Kennedys; but perhaps again only Jack could have done it: his brothers all had a touch of the roughneck. Even Jack himself apparently had his moments of feeling like an Irish outsider, but he was damned if he was going to show it.) Anyway, Nixon's entire campaign to date had hinged on his superior experience and know-how: and yet here he was peeping over at Jack as if *he* were the senior of the two.

As for Jack himself, memory has probably exaggerated his amused disdain. In fact he was probably just being himself, the same self he brought to bear on people as far apart as his brother Bobby and his soon-to-be vice president Lyndon Johnson: the look was just perceived differently in each case. With Nixon, I suppose he looked more or less the way the rest of us felt—slightly incredulous. At the end of one debate, he noticed that Nixon was still going through the motions of haranguing him after the mikes had been turned off, and he simply shook his head.

On my score card, Nixon actually won the debates by a small margin, largely because he argued more conscientiously throughout, while Kennedy at times seemed content to settle for rhetorical points ("Getting this country moving again" does not really constitute an argument).

But of course it didn't matter. Nixon had blown every single thing that counted, from the experience question to the name-recognition edge. It even seemed at the time as if Kennedy would turn out to be stronger with the Russians. (We didn't realize then that the Russians, *not* being eastern establishment, would pose no special problem for Nixon.) Finally, for those who still worried about it, I doubt if anybody even remembered that Kennedy *had* a father by the time the debates

---

FOLLOWING PAGES: On Thursday, July 14, the day after Kennedy won his party's nomination to be the Democratic standard bearer, he made a calculated and fateful decision that was to effectively and ultimately divide the United States for years to come— he nominated the Texas senator Lyndon Johnson to be his running mate. The nomination was not well received by many of Jack's own supporters, but Kennedy felt that he needed to win Texas if he was to win the election. His hunch proved correct. This photograph was taken at 4:30 that afternoon, shortly before Kennedy made his decision public.

were through. Kennedy's manhood could not have been more decisively established if he had gone up against Mr. Peepers.

From then on, the big excitement began to gather, the kind that builds in any kind of championship season. *By God, we're going to do it.* New arrivals on the bandwagon started, as they will, to act like first settlers. And Jack's appearance anywhere—especially, as I seem to recall, in open-topped cars—seemed to set off waves of sheer hysteria. Every day was V-J Day now. And the press recorded every loving moment of it because they liked Jack and Jack liked them, while Nixon had already developed all the press-relations panache of a Soviet official.

Considering which, the election seemed, to his fans at least, surprisingly close—a friendly count for Jack in Richard Daley's Chicago just offsetting a rumored one for Nixon in south Illinois. But being surprised by these things is a common mistake among fans, generated by their pernicious custom of talking only to one another.

From a broader perspective it should have been clear that the first Catholic victory would have to be a close one,* and that for various

*A daffy, eleventh-hour denunciation of the separation of Church and State by a long-forgotten Puerto Rican bishop is said to have played merry hell with JFK's late polls in heavily Protestant areas.

demographic reasons Northeasterners *as such,* from Thomas Dewey on, were in the process of becoming underdogs. Besides, 1960 was not a year of panic. Nothing *had* to be done about anything. Eisenhower had left everyone feeling pretty good, if benumbed, and I doubt if Kennedy picked up enough votes on my personal favorite, the boredom issue, to make a difference. And there really weren't that many other issues. Nixon was obviously not *against* getting America moving again. Kennedy made as much use as he decently could of a "missile gap," which turned out to be a fiction: but he had to use *something.*

But campaigns frequently contain a hidden content which comes bursting into view later. Cuba was perhaps the hottest item left, and naturally Kennedy used the hell out of it, little realizing how it would come back to haunt his presidency and perhaps even play a part in his death. At the time, it was just one more subject on which the candidates did not really disagree, and therefore had to exaggerate. What Nixon knew, but couldn't say (and the frustration must have nearly killed him), was that Eisenhower was already laying the groundwork for precisely the kind of response to Castro that Kennedy seemed to be calling for— namely, the Bay of Pigs invasion; a response

Kennedy, at the Los Angeles Coliseum, accepts the nomination in a speech which announces the New Frontier: "Give me your hand, your voice, your vote."

FOLLOWING PAGES: Frantic scenes like this one in Tazewell County, Illinois, became commonplace toward the close of the campaign.

that Kennedy, perhaps feeling bound and gagged by his own campaign rhetoric, and by whatever commitments Ike might have made to the Cuban exiles, would later follow through on so halfheartedly, to his own great misfortune. But of course we had no idea that any of that was latent in the apparently issueless campaign. The future is just a dream anyway as you whoop it up on election night. We only knew, in our barely sufficient numbers, that we wanted to see what the kid would do next.

Perhaps, though, old Joseph should be allowed the last word on the victory and the fulfillment of his lifelong dream. "I never could have done it," he said simply. For all his occasionally mind-boggling foolishness, the old man was not without his wisdom.

Kennedy arrives in Boston victorious, straight from the convention.

FOLLOWING PAGES: By the fall of 1960, the crowds of Kennedy admirers had grown to enormous size. Here, in Hartford, Connecticut, some 25,000 people came out to see their candidate.

73

THREE

The Kennedy Restoration

ould the young man wear a hat? For months now, Jack had stood convention on its ear, and reduced the hat industry to gibbering sobs, by going about the country hatless. In those days gentlemen wore hats everywhere, most especially to their own inaugurations, but there was simply no telling with this young rascal.

In the event, Jack did pop a black top hat on his head at the last moment, but something

By 11 A.M. on November 9, the morning after Election Day, the country had not yet made a decisive choice. Earlier, one of the network computers had predicted a landslide victory for Nixon, giving him 459 electoral votes against Kennedy's 78. John Chancellor, NBC's political guru, had predicted a Nixon sweep. But following these frightening and unexplained predictions, Kennedy had built up a 2,000,000-vote lead, only to see it dissolve to a 100,000-vote lead by the early morning hours—and Illinois, a key state, was still out. Finally, Richard Daley, a Kennedy ally and mayor of Chicago, pronounced Kennedy the winner in Illinois, a proclamation which resulted in charges of gross irregularities. But Nixon dropped his threat to order a recount, basically because his upstate Republican vote count was considered to be equally dubious. This photograph was taken in Bobby Kennedy's living room in Hyannis Port, Massachusetts, minutes before Daley's announcement on television.

jaunty about his style made it look like a comic prop and the whole reviewing stand like a Dickens illustration. Jack respected tradition, but wore it lightly: in line with which he also neglected to wear a topcoat on that rawest of Washington days, causing some to mutter "bravado" and "thermal underwear," while others murmured "youth" and "vigah." All the mutters and murmurs were correct: Jack was acting out, as in a charade, the arrival of a new generation in town.

Eisenhower knew what was going on all right, and he didn't seem to like it a bit. Pictures of him that day are most charitably described as pensive; it might be more accurate to say that he looked as if he was biting on a bullet dipped in lemon juice. As Jack drove off gaily with his young wife, defying the weather in an open-top car, one thought of poor Eisenhower, disconsolately hunched down and shrouded against the cold: the image might have passed for George Washington at Valley Forge for all its relevance on that day.

As for the address itself: read now in the ghostly light of Vietnam, it sounds like an unconscionable piece of saber-rattling, with its call for *infinite* (which is surely what the word "any" means) sacrifice in the cause of Liberty. But at the time, we were so inured to the sound of saber-rattling that it could have been the milkman clanking his bottles.

Critics have since read into the speech all of the famous Kennedy belligerence, which apparently the Kennedys can't help, but this interpretation tends to gloss over several contemporary realities.

My first impression back then was simply that Jack seemed to be enjoying a typical ride on his favorite speechwriter Ted Sorensen's rhetorical roller coaster, with its grandiose ups and downs, a style that almost *has* to go too far in order to achieve those sonorous contrasts. (Sorensen would later prove a great asset by collaborating with Jack on a single distinctive voice, or tongue, as opposed to the half dozen or so that most presidents speak in.)

But more to the point, a Democrat hardly *could* go too far in the direction of anti-Communism in the sour climate of the expiring fifties. Variously referred to as the party of appeasement and the party of treason over the last endless twelve years, the least its new representative could do now was glare and shake his fist. In this context, the bulk of the speech must have sounded suspiciously soft to a generation used to bomb shelters and air-raid drills. After all, it said nothing about evil empires or even mentioned the Russians by name, but instead used incendiary words like "negotiate" and "civility." It also talked about trumpets blown "but not to bear arms, although arms we need" (Sorensen drum roll). The real struggle from now on would be against "tyranny, poverty, disease, and war itself"—and in a passage that rang, and still rings faintly, throughout the Third World, it declared, "To those people in the huts and villages of half the globe, struggling to break the bonds of mass misery, we pledge our best efforts to help them help themselves." Saber-rattling should be made of sterner stuff than this.

The belligerence reading is important, though, because Belligerence Theory would later be used to explain so much of Kennedy's foreign policy, almost too handily. But no-body leaving the party that night, or the next morning, or even, as some did, the morning after that, supposed for a moment that he or she had been witnessing the advent of some mad warrior chieftain. If Kennedy was indeed subject to ungovernable fits of belligerence, the dreaded family curse, he certainly concealed it well in person—so well that even the wily Khrushchev took him for a softy when they met later in Vienna, and attempted outrageously to bully him.

As for the rest of us less wily ones, he simply seemed too well balanced, a strong man secure in his strength, to tip over too far in either direction. He also seemed like a very natural man in an artificial profession. Jack remains to this day perhaps the only politician who could ever stroll the sands hand-in-hand with his children without looking as if he'd rented the kids for the day. His pictures with Jackie and the family also seem completely unposed, partly because he *always* seemed unposed, almost unguarded, in fact, like a prizefighter who knows that his guard will take care of itself if needed.

And then there was Jackie. If there were indeed growing rifts between her and her husband over his alleged infidelities, she must have been an even better actor than he was, because she positively radiated happiness during those years to a degree surely quite unique among cheated wives. And then later, after Jack was gone, she positively outdid herself by weeping like a child over Camelot. It is hard to believe that those weren't awfully good years for her. Whatever Jack's putative sins, he must

On the porch at Bobby's house moments after the final victory was announced are JFK, Bobby, Jack's sister Eunice Shriver, and Pierre Salinger (with his back to the camera).

have found extraordinary ways to make it up to her—and clearly not just with gifts, which she was unusually adept at obtaining for herself.

For members of my generation, the scene of Jackie clambering clumsily over the death car to reach her dying husband in Dallas more or less clinched the matter, and pretty well put it out of bounds at the same time. She was doing exactly what we had been led to expect of her, and no actress who ever lived could have done it so convincingly.

One obvious but quite unusual thing that Jack did for his wife was simply not to stand in her way. Most presidents treat their wives only slightly better than their vice presidents, apportioning various good works to them in the Victorian manner, and basking in their adoring smiles when obtainable. Eleanor

Roosevelt, of course, created her own lime-light anyway, and Bess Truman flatly refused to play: but, with all exceptions noted, there has never been anything quite like Jackie in the White House.

For one thing, Jack himself never seemed to mind how much limelight his wife shared with him. If, as it turned out, *she* was the toast of France and not he, he appeared perfectly happy to take over the role of president's wife for the occasion. Perhaps because his ride to the top had been comparatively easy most of the way, or perhaps simply because big families don't let you get away with it, Jack never seemed to ooze ego like some presidents we have known, but, in this one respect at least, he behaved more like Mr. Reagan: confident enough to share the glory, knowing that there would always be plenty to go around. Even at home, Jackie never appeared to be "the little woman." In fact, she always seemed to be doing exactly what she wanted and having a whale of a time doing it: whether it was water skiing or learnedly explaining the White House paintings on TV.

In short, the "new kind of American" had brought with him to the presidency a new kind of wife, and a new kind of relationship to her. And much of the exhilaration of those years could finally be traced to the freewheeling nature of this partnership. It was almost as if

Jackie and Caroline, whose residence was soon to be changed to the White House, at home in Georgetown.

A victorious Jack Kennedy roams the grounds of the family compound in Hyannis Port, piggy-backing Caroline. The secret-service detail (background) *is in place.*

FOLLOWING PAGES: Of the many impossible tasks I performed during the Kennedy campaign, this one seemed insurmountable. The entire clan was scheduled to appear at the Hyannis Port armory, where the press was waiting for them. Joseph P. Kennedy was to appear for the first time in connection with the campaign. Euphoria reigned and I knew that this would be the only time to get the whole family together for a historic portrait. It took time and tremendous persuasion. Here, from left to right, are: Ethel Kennedy, Steve Smith, Eunice Kennedy Shriver, Jean Kennedy Smith, Rose Kennedy, Joe Kennedy, Sr., Jack Kennedy, Jackie, Bobby, Teddy, Pat Kennedy Lawford, Sargent Shriver, Joan Kennedy, and Peter Lawford in the library of Joe Sr.'s Hyannis Port house.

Nick and Nora Charles* had come to Washington: Jack and Jackie exuded a sense of adventure that one never quite got from Harry and Bess, let alone Dwight and Mamie.

People tend to have mixed feelings about the concept of a ceremonial presidency—especially when a given presidency seems to consist of nothing else. But in 1960, the country was parched for ceremony. After eight years of stag lunches at the White House and golfing weekends with businessmen and nothing but businessmen; or, to put it another way, after so many years of looking at John Foster Dulles—the country fairly craved color and gaiety.

As Arthur Schlesinger actually pointed out *before* the election, these historical patterns have a certain rhythmic inevitability to them. Eisenhower's favorite historical figure had been, you'll recall, Oliver Cromwell, who presided over the twelve gray years of the Puritan Protectorate in England during the 1640s and '50s. So after Cromwell's departure it was almost necessary to invent his successor, King Charles II, alias the Merry Monarch, to minister to the *other* side of the nation's personality: public sanity demands no less. And so it came to pass, exactly three hundred years later, that England's old colony suddenly found itself confronted with a merry president in its own right.

*The fun-loving, wisecracking couple in the *Thin Man* series.

Jack Kennedy was always aware of historical precedent (and if he wasn't, there was always Schlesinger on hand to remind him), but he also knew exactly how much of a Charles II-like Restoration the United States could take in 1960. He could not, for instance, very well bring back Maypoles or royal mistresses in open carriages: but he could give a boost to such quieter delights as poetry, as symbolized by Robert Frost's reading at the Inauguration, and music, and laughter—the latter by personal example.

Which brings us back to wit, the sine qua non of his career, the gift which made everything else possible. Charles II had also been a witty man (although after him, the British royal family hit a bit of a dry patch of roughly three hundred years and counting), and his wit must have lent a certain extra juice and flavor to *his* Restoration. A royal joke would presumably flow down through society like a healing tonic: and one imagines laughter breaking out in house after house, until all of London was lit with relief; it was all right to laugh now, humor had received the royal blessing.

It would be too much to claim quite so much for Jack Kennedy: but in our own great dispersion, humor at the top can provide a curious source of reassurance. Abraham Lincoln's jokes must have been a real source of strength and optimism during the Civil War,

Inauguration Day, January 20, 1961. Jack and Jackie leave their home on N Street for the last time.

and even FDR's more elephantine efforts helped put a smile on a nation at war. Yet despite its manifest value, we too have had precious few witty leaders—jokey ones, yes: but real wits tend to hurt too many feelings and make too many enemies on the way up; or else, like Adlai, to strike the voters at the last moment as somehow frivolous and unsound.

Jack as usual managed to dance between the pitfalls. His wit was seldom cruel and almost invariably genial—as if (as suggested in the previous chapter) designed originally for deflecting blows and defusing anger, while yielding no ground whatever: keep them laughing until you *have* to fight.

As for frivolity, I can only suggest that Kennedy must have been just a little better at being, or *seeming*, serious than Stevenson when the need arose. Maybe the constant pain in his back lent him a certain extra earnestness (history is made of such accidents) or perhaps it was a special air of intellectual urgency, sharpened by those endless debates at the Kennedy table. One stray piece of evidence may tell slightly in his favor on this. According to John Kenneth Galbraith, who knew both men intimately, Jack read a good five books to Adlai's one, which does not argue greater intelligence, to be sure, but possibly greater curiosity.

Anyway, Jack performed the rare Churchillian* double of being both funny and taken seriously at the same time, and we, in consequence, suddenly found ourselves blessed with possibly our first real presidential humorist in a hundred years. And we made the most of it. For too many years now, we had been obliged to make up our own jokes about Washington, out of such scratchy material as Eisenhower's press conferences (hilarious the first time), Mrs. Nixon's cloth coat, and Senator Joe McCarthy's operatic assaults on civility. There were probably young people alive at that very moment who didn't even know that a president *could* be witty: so Jack's first press conferences must have come as a blinding revelation to them, like sunshine in a rain forest.

And it wasn't just his one-liners. The same wand that Jack had waved over his family, turning them all into lovable cut-ups, he now waved over his whole administration, so that he even made his Harvard and Yale intellectuals seem sort of jolly (well, Galbraith and maybe Schlesinger were already—but McGeorge Bundy?). As if transformed by Jack's own style, middle-aged cabinet members seemed to turn into whiz kids in front of our eyes. No doubt their predecessors in the Eisenhower gang, such blithe spirits as Dulles and Sherman Adams and "Engine Charley" Wilson, made this trick slightly easier than it might have been. But Kennedy had a quite exceptional knack for attracting apparently vibrant people and then making them seem more so.

Not that official Washington now lacked for real whiz kids to go with the imitations. Jack, like his father Joe before him, had a gift for making public service seem like the most important and exciting thing in the world, and

*Jack was no Churchill, of course, and neither is anybody else. But in regard to his wit, as to so many other things, we had only three years in which to examine his work. The crucial point is that we expected, and eagerly looked forward to, something funny almost every time he opened his mouth.

suddenly the kind of youngbloods who today head straight for Wall Street seemed to be marching on the Capitol, demanding to know *right now* what they could do for their country. Kids who would now expect to start at $60,000 in pricey law firms were willing to sharpen pencils for peanuts in Bobby Kennedy's Justice Department; and indeed almost every government agency was enriched by such infusions. Washington is not generally known as a wildly stimulating city, but for three years it really swung, like a mansion that comes to life every hundred years, before returning to its sclerotic ways.

"Whom the gods love die young." There is no way of proving whether, if Jack had lived longer, he could have sustained anything like the excitement and sense of adventure that surrounded him in the first thousand days or so: we can only go with what we've got, which includes the one palpable fact that, unlike, say, Alexander the Great, he showed no signs of fading toward the end, but, if anything, quite the contrary. He smiled less than he used to, but this merely brought him up to par and made him look less boyish and more capable and *ready*. In fact, I suspect that, whatever they may think now, there were precious few Americans around at the time who didn't expect greater things of him right up to the end, as he continued to take the measure of his office: and so long as we hoped, the excitement was guaranteed.

But the excitement was by no means confined to the greater things: there were so many small pleasures to be had on the side in those years. For instance, previous presidents had

Jack Kennedy and Dwight Eisenhower leave the White House for the Capitol after a short conference, which included a discussion of the Bay of Pigs invasion.

tended to shy away from high culture as from a fence that might emasculate you on the way over. No red-blooded American voter would stand for it, they reckoned, in a man of the people ("Next thing you know, the feller'll be wearin' dresses"). Thus we had Roosevelt with his dismal "Home on the Range," and his Kate Smith; followed hotly by that accomplished pianist Harry Truman pounding out "The Missouri Waltz" over and over; he in turn to be followed by Eisenhower with his

Westerns and his practice putts in the Oval Office.

JFK made his own obeisances to the tradition by praising the James Bond books, but more than made up for that by inviting the likes of Pablo Casals to the White House: not just a highbrow, but a *foreign* highbrow. Jack even had the audacity to indicate that one might well start America moving again by getting it to listen to someone else's music for a change.

Once again, it was the wand that did it. In those days—and perhaps these too—the old cartoon version still held up everywhere: culture was something that American wives might occasionally drag their husbands to, but the latter didn't have to like it. But Kennedy positively seemed to relish it, as if he were signing a favorite bill into law. "I have never known anyone who listened more intently than he did," said Casals afterward.

Perhaps Jack sensed a stirring in the wind vis-à-vis sexual roles, or perhaps his confidence in his own manhood was such that he believed he could even take up knitting and get away with it. Whatever it was, he somehow made culture seem like yet another lark, part of the wave of high spirits that was sweeping Washington and the nation. And the public appeared to go for it as it has never quite gone

for Ronald Reagan's later restoration of corn. I suppose you had to be there—but old Pablo and his cello, with Stravinsky still to come, actually seemed like a much merrier idea than any number of rock groups or aging movie stars have seemed since.

And as with Culture, so with Intellect, another subject that Anglo-American pols have generally preferred to approach with rubber gloves and fire tongs. Characteristically, Jack managed to blow much of the dust and cobwebs off this venerable monster with one immortal wisecrack, aimed at a group of Nobel winners who'd dropped in on the White House, as eggheads tended to do in those days (Ike would probably have fled to his putting green). Jack simply called them "the most extraordinary collection of talent, of human knowledge" ever to grace the place, "with the possible exception of when Thomas Jefferson dined alone." Note once again the art of it: by bringing in Jefferson, he was bringing in the American people, and giving us a new insight from homespun material into what intellect actually does. And so the windows were opened, and the monster wasn't a monster after all.

Yet another unlikely subject that Kennedy made positively hilarious was exercise. This has since become a grim business indeed, as you can tell from the sheer number of books

Inauguration Day—January 20, 1961. On that bitterly cold day, the young president pronounced his vision of sacrifice and service to the country. A change indeed from the dreary Cold War–dominated years of the Eisenhower/John Foster Dulles administration.

The country's leadership leaves Capitol Hill, where the inaugural address was given.

about it, or simply by looking into the crazed eyes of joggers. But Jack made it funny almost immediately by getting his little brother Bobby to do it for him, instead of doing it himself. We now know that this was a counsel of necessity: Jack had to conceal his bad back even more craftily than FDR concealed his legs. But at the time all we saw was a president smiling seraphically at his desk while Bobby ran and ran and did his best to grin through the pain.

As usual, the exercise thing wasn't just a joke: if it had been, it wouldn't have lasted five minutes. But Kennedy needed only one look at the nation's youth, and statistics pertaining thereto, to see that asking it to bear any burden or make any sacrifice was already a sick joke.* The fifties had been *the* decade of the automobile: with Eisenhower's beaming approval, highways had begun to spin out across the nation like interlocking spider webs, and suddenly people didn't even have to run to catch the train anymore, because there wasn't any train. Social critics conjectured that American legs might eventually retract altogether, while American bellies ballooned out further and further to hide the remains.

Since Kennedy had indeed pledged himself to getting the country moving again, it seemed a wise idea to start out by taking it one American at a time. But mere words would never have budged us off our car cushions, any more than they later got us to "whip inflation now"

or any of the other edifying things we are periodically asked to do; and it's awfully hard to think of any other president who could have done it through personal, or even brotherly, example. Jerry Ford, for instance, would just have seemed silly, and nobody would have noticed Jimmy Carter. Richard Nixon might actually have set exercise back a piece. But Kennedy had created around himself an exceptional, and unrepeatable, situation: if his family did something it was automatically fun—but also well worth doing oneself. The Kennedy ensemble had somehow become a model of how to balance seriousness with play— because Jack himself did, and he had re-created the rest of them in his own public image. After that, it merely required a few snapshots of them frolicking at Hyannis Port to confirm the illusion—even if, up close, the Kennedys appeared to be trying awfully hard to break one another's legs.

Of course, when you stop to think about it, a family that seems to have nothing better to do with its spare time than play touch football all day, and push people into swimming pools, doesn't sound as if it has an awful lot to teach anyone; but Jack swept it all up—exercise, practical jokes, high-spirited family, and venerable cellists alike—into a sense of bubbling movement and rebirth.

Such a program, if you can call it that, sounds terribly time-consuming; but it wasn't particularly. Jack knew that in the image business, you only have to start things rolling and look in on them occasionally, and the media will take care of the rest. The only requirement is that you have to give those media

*Jack didn't have to look even that far to know how hard it is to demand sacrifices of a flawed body. Jack's obsession with fitness may well have been inspired originally by his own spinal column.

something to work with. For instance, even the friendlier press corps of those times (which seems to have concealed almost more stories than it broke) had not been able to do much for the Roosevelt, Truman, or Eisenhower clans: Margaret Truman's singing and, of course, the mere fact of Eleanor, were about all the story they could find, and they devoted absolutely all the space they decently could to both subjects. But for the Kennedys there was suddenly never enough space, and they didn't have to hustle for it—so long as, to repeat, Jack looked in occasionally.

As for the time involved—all presidents have wasted time, and in most cases *really* wasted it. Eisenhower spent so much time on the links that his famous campaign slogan about going to Korea was unofficially changed to "If elected, I shall go to Washington." Truman whiled away his spare moments playing poker with his cronies (the word has never fit a group better) and doing a little manly cussin' on the side (a *Time* reporter who dropped by couldn't believe his ears). Reagan, I believe, cuts wood, an activity associated with the very sound of sleep. All in all, Kennedy wasted vastly less time than our two most popular postwar presidents, Ike and Ronald Reagan, gave more press conferences than anyone since FDR, and read more on the side than any of them except maybe Truman, while tackling an agenda that must have consumed either mountains of time or exhausting minutes of concentration or both.

It's just that when Jack *did* waste time, it tended to add a little something to the gaiety of nations. This something has since been temporarily and partially eclipsed by our *other*

Jack Kennedy dons his silk hat for one brief, shining moment.

favorite subject—namely, Marilyn Monroe and her putative connections with the Kennedys, mainly Bobby. When poor Marilyn croaked out her unforgettable "Happy Birthday, Mr. President" at Madison Square Garden back in 1963, we took it to be just the latest caprice from the fun-loving Restoration Court of the Merry President.

But in the current murk, that evening seems positively tragic. Viewed today on videotape, and with hindsight, it becomes painfully clear that Miss Monroe was already so wasted by pills and anxiety that simply getting through that least demanding of songs must have been

93

a screaming torture for her. Unfortunately, we didn't know about drugs back then: or at least not enough to see them everywhere we turned. People could still be overcome by honest emotion in those days, without everyone demanding a blood test, and I guess Marilyn could *just* have passed for honestly emotional and nothing but.

Afterward, Jack walked up to her, smiling, and gossip has practically turned this walk into a tryst as we rewatch it now, although to this day I don't know what else he should have done. To us, it was just one of hundreds of gracious moments in his calendar: but all the other moments have been dimmed in memory by our national obsession with the late Monroe—an obsession which (all hands at least agree on this) Jack did not share.

In any event, whatever happened or didn't happen in real life pales beside the myths that have grown up around it since. Marilyn's death left almost as many questions open as Jack's would, and from that night on the Monroe legend has grown and changed as good legends will, putting it on an eventual gossip collision course with the Kennedy legend. Over the years, Marilyn has proved an irresistible subject for writers between books; and any character who has been sifted through the various talents of Norman Mailer, Gloria Steinem, Truman Capote—and how many others?—will never be quite the same. So I for one will

Jack sported his silk hat throughout the inaugural parade. The parade lasted more than four hours, but the young president enjoyed the spectacle and stayed to the bitter end.

never feel quite certain whether she really was the eternal and invariable victim, or whether she just occasionally, and in a most victimlike manner, went out and got exactly what she wanted.

Beyond the further obvious observation that few men in any walk of life, including the ministry, could easily have resisted Miss Monroe under full sail, I have little to add to the current salacious hum of speculation except my own mild regret that this lovely broken creature seems posthumously and by sheer inadvertence to have done as much over the last few years to block and darken the view of the president she idolized as all the political revisionists put together.

In tedious reality, even the most sedulous carpet sniffers have never come anywhere near establishing a significant romance between Jack and Marilyn, because there simply wasn't the time or the logistical opportunity. (The book on Bobby may be less clear—I just don't know. But what keeps that end of the story alive is the piquant possibility that for once the brother who "just didn't do that kind of thing" did, while the brother who *did* that kind of thing *didn't*. If you can follow all that.)

People who like their history served that way will always find goodies in any period. But in sober fact, the whole Monroe question could only have occupied a fractional place in Jack's thoughts, which were everywhere else at the time, circling the globe restlessly, endlessly: people who picture Jack scheming his life away in saucy melodramas should take a look sometime at his average work week. Even the royal family hasn't got *that* kind of time. Girls were presumably for distraction, and perhaps for quick boosts of confidence (of which Jack may have had a little less than he seemed), and there's no reason to think Jack ever offered them anything more.

Anyhow, even the view from 1988 isn't all clouds, because too many people were there and *remember*—and have, one trusts, passed the memory on like an electric current. (I've encountered that kind of charge from people who knew Churchill, so I know it is possible.) And one thing these witnesses surely remember is that the Kennedy excitement had nothing whatever to do with Marilyn Monroe, or even with girls—whom I'll get to *en masse* and *tout en court* (if you'll allow a little creative French) a little later—or even, in the last resort, with sideshows, delightful as those might have been.

In fact, precisely what made the sideshows delightful was the sense that they were merely sparks off a dynamo, a joyous overflow of energy from the red-hot center. Kennedy created the impression that anything could happen in this world and beyond, and that everything was being considered, and this was at the very heart of the fun.

During those wonderful days of inaugural celebrations, Jackie firmly established her position as the international style setter. Her hairstyle, her clothes, her every move would be imitated throughout the world.

How far he delivered on all this, or how far *any* modern president can deliver on such things, will be discussed in my next chapter. But bringing his countrymen back to life, after the twilight sleep of the fifties, would have been no small feat in itself, even if done completely with mirrors.

The author of *Why England Slept* was obviously an ardent believer in morale as such, and in the sheer national energy that it generates. Insofar as this is so (and history is peppered with corroborating examples) JFK vaults over several worthy but soporific presidents to a very high place indeed.

Revisionists may revise the rest of Kennedy until they're blue in the face and until there's no monument left; but even the surliest of them has never suggested, or reasonably could, that it wasn't great to be alive in those years. And, to put the matter as temperately as possible, it isn't every administration that can claim that, or anything remotely close to it.

P.S. Incidentally, whatever else there may have been in Washington, D.C., or even Hollywood, there was only one woman in Camelot, and her name was Jacqueline; and she knew it and wept.

Jacqueline Kennedy on the porch at the house in Hyannis Port.

FOUR

Achievements and Possibilities

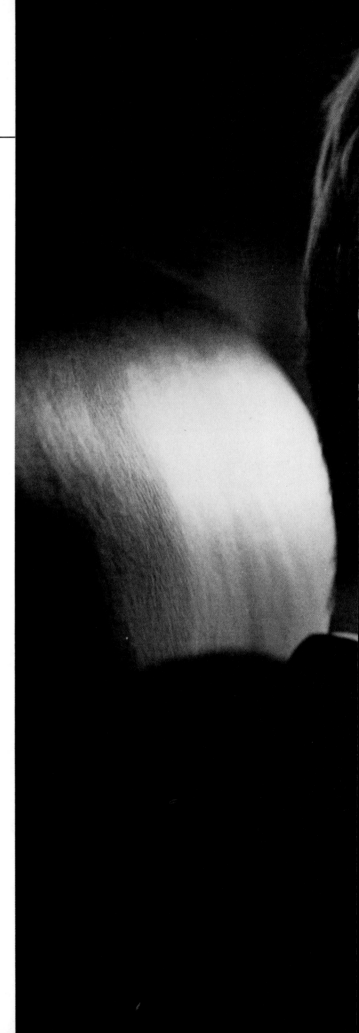

Jack Kennedy's performance as president has, by this time, been so thoroughly ransacked and mulled over by professional historians that the enthusiastic amateur finds himself left with the genial luxury of taking just a few central strands and holding them up to what he trusts is a new light. So what follows is not so much a strict historical account (far from it) as a species of meditation designed to trigger counter-meditations on the reader's part.

To get the dull part over with first, and quickly: the first and most abiding shock for *any* freshman president, however well he has cushioned himself for it, is discovering how little he is actually free to do. Domestically, he finds himself tied down from the start, like Gulliver, by a gossamer network of special interests and prior commitments. And the one thing he *does* seem free to do is quite illusory: he is free to spend money to his heart's content, right up to the limits of current popularity (see Reagan's budgets). On the other hand, any attempt to *cut* the budget will be met with implacable resistance, even if the president's name is Reagan, but raise it he may—until his own expenditures form themselves into fresh little chains, with brand new

lobbies and interest groups settling on them overnight like rust. As everybody knows, nothing in Washington is more indestructibly enduring than a temporary program.

I bring up these dismal economic verities, which are usually best accompanied by lumpy-looking charts, not handsome photos, only to mention that Kennedy handled them adroitly, thus buying himself precious freedom to maneuver. In fact our particular Gulliver succeeded at various times in actually balancing the budget, while cutting taxes slightly and controlling both inflation and unemployment to a point that seems utopian today. These were, of course, still prosperous days for the American imperium, and Eisenhower had, in this respect at least, left behind a decent little legacy. Jack saw no major reason to meddle with it much, to the mighty annoyance of fiscal liberals, who accused him of being a businessman's president in disguise. But Jack obviously saw no burning reason to spend money before he got his programs, and no way of getting his programs if he couldn't pay for them to at least some extent: he wasn't *that* popular yet.

"May you live in interesting times" goes the old Chinese curse, and in the matter of economics dullness is often the absolute best you can hope for: in which case Kennedy was, for once in his life, perfectly willing to be as dull

The first cabinet meeting. The president is in his customary place framed by the flags of the United States and of his office. The vice president sits opposite and the president is flanked by the secretaries of state and the treasury.

103

THE
PRESIDENT
JAN 20 1961

as the worst of them.* He even managed somehow to tiptoe between the mini-recessions and microscopic inflation scares which had pockmarked the Eisenhower administration. Between them, in fact, Ike and Jack had built so well that, ironically, the middle-class hell-raisers of the late sixties might never have felt half so free to frolic if they weren't convinced that our economoy was impregnable and could meet their demands and support their shenanigans forever.

When it comes to foreign affairs, the simile of the Iron Maiden or straitjacket may come closer than Gulliver's tiny problems to describing a new president's plight: The restraining garment in question was fashioned originally by the Truman Doctrine in 1947, which grandly committed America to resist aggression anywhere in the globe that we deemed fit—a commitment which unfortunately could not be retired with Mr. Truman and the very different world he confronted. Ever since then, presidents have either squirmed quietly in the policy jacket, as Kennedy presumably did, or have attempted to strut in it like Reagan—but they have all been stuck with the thing. Which

*In economics even more than other matters of state, a president's genius consists chiefly of hiring the right advisers and understanding what they're talking about. If he also knows how to apply it to political realities, he is a *real* genius.

The first Joint Chiefs of Staff meeting in the cabinet room at the White House. General Lyman Lemnitzer (right) *is the chairman of the Joint Chiefs. Facing the president are general Thomas D. White (Air Force), Admiral Arleigh "Thirty-Knot" Burke (Navy), and General George Decker (Army). On the agenda, the Bay of Pigs.*

The president meets with leaders of both houses, including Senate majority leader Everett Dirksen, Senators Hubert Humphrey and George Smathers, and House majority leader John McCormack and minority leader Joe Martin.

means that, for the last forty years, no swallow has been allowed to fall anywhere, whether in Angola or Laos or Sri Lanka, without our demanding to know whether it fell or was pushed—by the Communists, of course. All the world's a domino game, and we can never leave the table.

Kennedy was not spared this curious burden of office in the least. His stint in the White House witnessed at least the usual amount of lunatic aggression in the world, and the wonder is how seldom he allowed us to get wastefully involved in it. Although the situation he had landed in required an awful lot of police work, he was determined to keep it small and to exploit instead our own indubitable edge

over the Russians—namely, that if we play our cards, or dominoes, right, we are simply more attractive allies for most people to have than they are.

Kennedy realized at once what most presidents never do, that there are many initiatives open overseas that have nothing whatever to do with aggression or the power to wage war, and that it might even be possible someday to conduct a whole foreign policy which does not rely on either U.S. intervention (or the threat of it) or massive bribery as the only cards in our hand. We know from his speeches and other papers that Kennedy had scores of such initiatives in mind (one thinks fondly of Food for Peace, although either the word "peace"

or the word "progress" was implicit in all his pet ones), but perhaps the two most famous are the Alliance for Progress with South America and the Peace Corps, both of which illustrate as well as anything how *differently* from other politicians Kennedy saw the world.

In both cases, the ideas had been kicked around before, but mainly as vague aspirations. Better relations with Latin America was one of those pretty ideas, like helping the Indians, that floats up in every generation. Franklin Roosevelt's Good Neighbor policy even went so far as to change the name of Sixth Avenue in New York to Avenue of the Americas, to please our friends to the south: but even the new name never really took hold, and the policy was one more sad victim of World War II.

After the war, Latin affairs returned pretty much to business as usual, which means, in effect, lordly indifference punctuated by spasms of alarm. (Somebody *else* interested in our pet continent? How dare they!) Although the Latin countries have never exactly been our colonies, our lack of real, passionate interest in them has something quasi-colonial about it, resembling in its way the British attitude to, say, Australia (I've never met an educated Englishman who wanted to go there), or the French to Algeria. In practical terms, our ideal Latin American government seemed to be either a democracy backed by a military regime, or,

if necessary, an outright military regime which occasionally allowed free elections: within that range, we could deal with anybody!

The success of this policy, if that's the word for it, can be gauged by the sheer quantity of fruit thrown at Richard Nixon during the epic swing down there in 1958. The locals were convinced in those days that our entire interest in Latin America devolved upon the fortunes of the United Fruit Company, so Nixon's welcoming committee was merely making sure that some of their fruit at least would never make it into the company cans.

On rereading Kennedy's senatorial speeches, I am struck by how well he had used those "idle" hours on the Hill to travel abroad and to prepare foreign policy positions that he could later follow up on as president, thus sparing us some of the agonies of "on-the-job training," which young presidents inevitably put us through; and Latin America was no exception. By good chance he had actually spent some time in Argentina as a youth, and he seemed to have a real feel for the continent plus a most uncommon belief in its importance.

Before taking the oath, he had already set up contact with Adolf Berle, the architect of the old Good Neighbor policy, to see how much of that could be reclaimed and updated. But the times had changed. Once upon a time, a revolution in the subcontinent simply meant

A restless president, on his way from the cabinet room to the Oval Office, quickly glances at the papers to catch up on the news.

that one military junta had replaced another, frequently overnight so as not to disturb anyone, while the fruit flowed on. So the Good Neighbors we dealt with always turned out to be a lot like the ones who'd just left. But now a revolution could mean the real thing: a popular rising against the *whole* ruling class: this year's junta, last year's junta, and all. Fidel Castro had demonstrated for all to see how an army trained largely to compete in horse shows might be a poor match for a popular leader with something more serious on his mind and a gang of combat-trained romantics at his side. Which suddenly meant that the question "Who is thy neighbor?" had to be answered over and over before we could have any policy at all.

The lesson had already been learned rudely enough by Ike when he reached out clumsily and attempted to embrace Castro at the last moment, only to be rebuffed by the commandante before he even got inside the door. Castro also proceeded to complicate matters for us, then and forever, by revealing himself as a closet Marxist who could not be wooed by anything. After that, the question was: Could any insurgency be trusted? Our conservative mainstream said, quite understandably, no: all revolutions in Latin America were inherently anti-American, because we and our business interests were always part of the problem; and if anti-American, the rising must also be pro-Communist, because even a radical government needs a friend, preferably a big one.

Kennedy did not agree with the second half of this thesis (the pro-Communist bit) at all, and thought that something could be done about the first half (the anti-American bit) as well. As one of our few genuinely cosmopolitan presidents, he knew from personal experience that countries differ not only one from the other, but from county to county, hill to valley, outback to shore, and he refused to believe that this whole mass of jangling entities, known for convenience as Latin America, craved freedom solely in order to hand itself over to Cuba, or Moscow, or anyone else.

Thus he saw no point in thrusting ourselves forward once more as patrons to people who were sick to death of patrons. Instead he made it his business to search out and encourage (with our eyes open this time) potential popular leaders who wanted no foreign overlords whatsoever, not even us, and then to help these leaders form a natural buffer against Castro and whatever else was out there. In this Jack was willing to take unusual chances, despite the dread example of Cuba. The prospects for the new alliance suggested that our new friends did not even have to be friends in

At a reception in the Blue Room of the White House, Kennedy sports a Band-Aid. The source of the injury remains unknown.

111

Kennedy's easy style was set by his demeanor. Here, leaving the Oval Office through the back door to the rose garden, he is accompanied by the vice president and followed by aides Ted Sorensen and Larry O'Brien. To the chagrin of the secret-service detail assigned to him, he often left that way when going to impromptu meetings.

a personal sense: the alliance only prescribed that we be able to work together toward the goal of development—then we'd see. Otherwise, they could even be socialist if they wanted. The hemisphere is large enough "to have diverse social systems in different countries," advised Kennedy's task force, and besides, *"private enterprise . . . is not the determining principle or sole objective of American policy"* (italics mine). The only absolutes that we insisted on were "unequivocal support to democracy and opposition to dictatorship."

There followed a list of extremely detailed economic suggestions, which again belong in the land of charts, but which collectively added up to a species of Marshall Plan for our Third World subcontinent, along with a pledge to improve the quality of our ambassadors down there in order to implement it—men who would henceforth, ideally, know and care a little bit about the countries they were posted to. All this and more was to be the special project of one of Kennedy's most brilliant protégés, Dick Goodwin, who personally scouted twenty-two Latin countries to see what needed doing in *each one.*

What is both revealing and saddening is how eagerly so many Latin Americans accepted the whole package. It was the first real token of concern from Big Brother in a long, long time. Even before the terms had taken form, the Latin Americans believed in Jack wholeheartedly as virtually the reincarnation of FDR; and when Jack went down there on a couple of flying visits, his uproarious reception was the mirror opposite of Nixon's, as if he came from an entirely different country. Which in a sense he did.

Soon after Jack's death, the air went out of the Alliance, just like that. Lyndon Johnson promptly signed on *Eisenhower's* old adviser to the area, Thomas Mann, who presumably helped his new master decide that the Dominican Republic (which had been one of Jack's pet projects) was turning much too far left, and that it was high time to send some of our troops somewhere anyway (LBJ's loyalty to the Kennedy legacy stopped at the water's edge). And later on still, the leftist government of Salvador Allende in Chile would be destabilized to death by the CIA, which had never had so much fun under Kennedy.

It could simply be that the Alliance was always too good to be true, and that it contained the fatal flaw of Kennedy programs in general—i.e., that it needed a Kennedy. At any rate, it needed one for a little while longer than it got. Three-years-minus was, according to Goodwin, barely time to set up the machinery, in the teeth of the usual bureaucratic stall. But with *five* more years, say, Kennedy's personal friendships down there, involving such men of the future as Figueres of Costa Rica,

Betancourt of Venezuela, and Muñoz-Marin of Puerto Rico, would surely have been implemented by enough others to form a *cordon sanitaire* capable of cooling things when they appeared to overheat, without resorting to troops or spooks. Once again, the key was Kennedy's private assessment of political talent, and the clock had to run out on that eventually. But if the structure he had envisaged had at least gone up halfway, it is hard to believe that such a masterpiece of mutual incomprehension as the great Central American muddle of today could ever have reached its current state of chaos and menace.

Last, but not least, he had the wit to understand that trade with a prosperous left-wing government can prove at least as profitable as trade with a repressive one that banks in Switzerland and lets too much of its manpower rot in poverty. Jack was never anti-business, although he did allow in one heated moment that "my father was right. All businessmen are sons of bitches." In hindsight Kennedy's Latin policies may actually seem almost dangerously left-wing, yet there was no massive conservative opposition to them at the time, and the liberals remained, incredibly, suspicious. Jack's tendency to play politics by ear would in fact keep both sides off-stride to this day.

In the matter of Latin America, Kennedy's legacy* consists mainly of a memory and a possibility. After his death, we returned clunkily and one more time to business as usual down there: that crabbed, unimaginative non-policy with which we came in. And South

*I am omitting for now actual increases in prosperity that may have been spinoffs of the *Alianza*, because there are too many other possible contributing factors.

Kennedy talking to Secretary of State Dean Rusk and Richard Bissell.

The Bay of Pigs was the first serious crisis of the Kennedy years. It came early in his administration and a shaken president took the blame. "There is an old saying that victory has a hundred fathers but defeat is an orphan. I am the responsible officer of the government." But in a later aside, he added, "All my life I've known better than to depend on the experts. How could I have been so stupid as to let them go ahead?" Here, seated from left to right, are Secretary of Defense Robert McNamara; chairman of the Joint Chiefs, Lyman Lemnitzer; CIA director Allen Dulles; and deputy director Richard Bissell. In the foreground at the left are the president's military aid General Chester "Ted" Clifton and Walt Rostow, deputy to McGeorge Bundy (hidden left), the president's national security adviser. This is one of their last meetings prior to the invasion. Bissell in the end was identified as the architect and mastermind of the Bay of Pigs fiasco.

Americans went back, presumably, to resenting us. However, when, to this very day, Latin democrats decide to try really hard to think of something that's nice about America, they think about Jack, and maybe about Jimmy Carter, who tried to pick up some of the strands, and about what might have been.

So long as our presidents continue to be essentially domestic creatures who have to look up the names of new countries before they can send our troops there, most of these dreams must remain where they came from, in Camelot.

As for the Peace Corps, one can just imagine the pre-Kennedy conversations. "Wouldn't it be nice to mobilize our boys for peace instead of war for a change, George?" "Sure, Gracie, and equip them all with olive branches and harps, right?"

Mobilizing our boys for anything at all has always proved excruciatingly difficult. Under the stress of the Depression, FDR did manage to mobilize some of them for peaceful purposes, but strictly domestic ones. Abroad was somebody else's problem. Perhaps because we feel we've left all that behind, Americans have seldom been deeply interested in other countries; probably not one in ten of us, even now, could draw a plausible map of Central America or even Vietnam. And as for foreign languages—doesn't everyone else speak English by this time?

To ask the children of such a culture, in the very heyday of *The Affluent Society*, to abandon their pursuit of gray flannel and upward mobility in order to live and work in the kinds of places that even travel agents won't touch—places where English is not, in fact, spoken and air conditioning is as rare as a square meal—must have seemed even more impractical than usual in sleek, prosperous 1960: yet Kennedy asked it and got it.

Americans old enough to be in politics habitually underestimate the idealism and curiosity of the nation's youth, and consequently never even bother to call upon it—with the consequence that whole generations go to their graves never knowing what they could have done, or what was in them. But in the Kennedy years, nobody had that excuse anymore. Not everybody joined the Peace Corps, of course—it really *was* kind of impractical for most people—but the same can-do impulse began to drive many young people into civil rights or the domestic Peace Corps, or local government, or anything that could be moved. In fact, the number of outstanding congressmen, et al., who entered politics precisely because of Kennedy would continue to keep his ideals in circulation for years after his death. Governor Michael Dukakis, who was one of them, recently reminded us of the title these youngsters answered to—"Children of the New Frontier": a sunny phrase from a sunny time.

The president in the Oval Office. The windows face the rose garden.

And so it came about that, for a rare moment in our history, grown-ups actually stopped calling their kids lazy or selfish or silent, and indeed by halfway through the decade many grown-ups wished only that they could go back to calling them all those things. But before the idealism exploded in a cloud of pot and childishness in the late sixties, and went spinning, leaderless, off the rails and into interior space, we had a unique chance to see what young Americans could do for their fellow man, if anybody ever asked them. (It was also a decade in which making huge sums of money strictly for yourself went out of style, and some old-timers feared that it would never come back. They needn't have worried.)

What was doubly unusual about this sudden spume of idealism was how down-to-earth practical most of it was: it was not just about forming discussion groups, but about going straight to the spot. Jack Kennedy never believed in motion for its own sweet sake, or in any form of meaningless bustle. His favorite quotation apropos of this was Lord Falkland's: "If it is not necessary to change, it is necessary *not* to change." ("If it ain't broke, don't fix it.") So his programs all concerned things that needed fixing.

The Peace Corps preeminently was about something that needed fixing. We were by that time well into the era of the Ugly American, that legendary minor U.S. diplomat who knows little and cares less about the countries where he's stationed, and Graham Greene's quiet one, who never really leaves home at all, but sees every foreign country as so much raw material which might, if the natives are very lucky and we are very good, become just like America someday.

In short, the rest of the world badly needed to meet some Americans who didn't wear uniforms or even business suits, and who didn't retreat into embassies in their free time, while *this* country desperately needed a pool of young people who could cut the cord the way their ancestors had, and live like natives themselves until they actually knew how to think like them. If any of Jack's global dreams, such as the Alliance for Progress itself, were ever to come true he would need such personnel in a hurry and for a long time.

Like so many topics in this book, this one runs slap into the question "What if?" Without Kennedy's dreams, who needed his new personnel? Although the Corps in the years since then has turned out enough distinguished graduates to justify itself many times over, if only as a great finishing school, it has not notably enriched our recent diplomacy. Interestingly, though, the Peace Corps has remained popular under far less idealistic presidents, proving itself a sturdy enough idea to survive just about anything. So if ever we get ourselves another Jack Kennedy—an apparition we are constantly being promised by coltish young Democrats—he will find at least

At a meeting on domestic policy, Kennedy chats with aide Ted Sorensen (hidden).

Kennedy addresses a congressional delegation in the Oval Office while Lyndon Johnson looks on.

one of the old tools still at hand and ready for use. But for now, the legacy of both the Corps and the *Alianza* consists chiefly of the lesson.

Jack Kennedy really knew and cared about foreign countries as one cares about personal friends. Other presidents have been just as interested in foreign policy, but that's different. Richard Nixon loved moving the big pieces about the board, but nobody ever supposed he *cared*: the pawns certainly didn't. Woodrow Wilson cared about Humanity and the big picture, but he never knew much about Serbs and Croats, or Czechs and Slovaks, whom he helped lump together in such unmanageable combinations immediately after World War

I. So Kennedy remains far and away the best example of what a president might hope to accomplish who has not had his perspective hopelessly narrowed, as by a pencil sharpener, by the ceaseless pressures of domestic politicking. As a superpower, as we like to call ourselves, and leader of the free world to boot, we urgently need a superpresident, a leader of worlds, not districts; so it is sobering to realize that since we *became* a superpower at the end of World War II, we have come close (no more than one and perhaps two half-times) with Kennedy, Nixon, and Carter, respectively.

"Ask not what your country can do for you, but what you can do for your country." Kennedy and Sorensen really rang a bell, a school bell to be precise, with that one. Bright young people came storming into Washington to ask that very question.

On certain fronts—civil rights, for instance—Kennedy's young constituents actually bounded out in front of him, partly because even he could move only at the speed of politics, but partly because, in this particular field, his brother Bobby seems to have been out in front of him too. A story is told that when Martin Luther King was jailed during the election campaign of 1960, Jack called up Coretta King to condole, but Bobby called the judge and got Dr. King released. So perhaps it is fair to picture Jack looking to Bobby for his leads on civil rights, even as the kids looked to him. Anyway, one way or the other, the kids knew soon enough what the brothers wanted. They saw Attorney General Bobby defy Governor Ross Barnett in the matter of James Meredith, the first black to register at the University of Mississippi, or "Ole Miss," and later they saw Jack welcome Martin Luther King to Washington, and perhaps they also noted that blacks polled in mid-1963 listed Jack just behind King himself as having done the most for Negro rights. So while Kennedy couldn't very well join in the Great Marches himself, he was felt to be there.

The speed of politics was another matter. As noted, Kennedy had never learned to be a real parliamentarian (though he got better at it as his presidency went along), and even with such a gifted one at his side as Lyndon Johnson

ready to help out (and, unlike his entourage, Jack really respected Lyndon), he had a tough time getting anything much through Congress, let alone the kind of sweeping Civil Rights Bill that Bobby was urging and would soon (1963) actually be drafting. Relations with the Hill are never easy for any first-term president sitting on an eyelash of a mandate. But on top of that, most of the key committees were still presided over by conservative southerners, sworn to frustrate any civil-rights-prone president.

What Jack was waiting for was, of course, the landslide that Lyndon actually got. With that kind of mandate, his relations with the Hill would have improved like a charm, parliamentary mistakes or no, and some at least of Lyndon Johnson's Great Society would, for better or worse, have been Jack Kennedy's whatchamacallit (Jack would have had his own name for it). In fact, Lyndon got much of it through Congress *because* it was felt to be Jack's—his hold on the Hill having been miraculously strengthened by death.

Anyway, the missing, or misplaced, mandate is what makes Kennedy's presidency so tantalizingly hard to assess on a nuts-and-bolts basis. (I'm assuming here that he would have gotten the mandate, although this seemed far from certain on, say, November 21, 1963: anyway it's a pretty good bet that he would have won by *something*.) The questions multiply. Would a second-term Jack, with nothing to lose, have succeeded in ramming so much social legislation through Congress, or did it indeed take his death to win it the extra votes? Would he have *wanted* quite so much social legislation quite so fast as Johnson, who came to see it as the particular jewel in his own crown? Above all, would Jack have expanded to potential infinity a war whose hidden costs eventually beggared the Great Society and left many Americans devoutly determined never to try another one?

The Vietnam question keeps forcing itself to the front of the line, though it belongs further back. A couple of his close friends have testified that Jack actually intended to use the "mandate" to wind down the war posthaste before it really got going (at that point, American support amounted to not much more than a foot in the door). But if so, it is too bad that these friends did not convey Jack's intentions more urgently to LBJ.

Unfortunately, a politician's private remarks are usually next to worthless as evidence, but there are several reasons, based on other patterns in his performance, which we'll get to in a moment, to believe he would have tried *something*. And the first and simplest one that meets the eye is that Jack was extremely cost-conscious. In view of his miraculous double of lowering taxes and balancing the budget, it seems unlikely on the face of it that he would have spent the country into bankruptcy over a war that made so little sense intellectually. Unlike his sly, big-handed successor, he knew exactly the cost of both guns and butter, and he would never have tried to hide a whole war from the nation's bookkeepers.

So, had Kennedy lived, it would surely have been guns or it would have been butter, but not both, and knowing his commitment to social betterment at home and filling stomachs abroad, and his somewhat cooler view of Southeast Asia, it is hard to see him throwing out the butter.

But what about his famous belligerence? I suppose the quickest answer to this might be to ask the Cuban exiles in Florida. As far as they were and are concerned, Jack's failure to provide air cover for the Bay of Pigs operation marked him forever as either the greatest coward or the greatest villain who ever lived, preferably both.

The whole Bay of Pigs episode has been much written about and puzzled over. But its bearing on Jack's eagerness to commit American soldiers abroad seems clear enough. And if he wouldn't use a handful of our men to ensure a popular victory ninety miles from home, it passes easy belief that he would have used half a million of them to attain an unlikely and not overwhelmingly popular victory half a world away, machismo or no machismo (we'll take a look at that red herring in due time).

Beyond that, the Bay of Pigs raises questions, as so many things do, about Jack's legacy from Eisenhower. Recent historians have tended to apply Teflon to Ike after the fact, even as they strip it off Jack, so one can hardly

That look could bode disaster. Kennedy's visitor, a senator asking for special considerations on behalf of his state, left empty-handed.

analyze one without the other. Thus Ike was against any "land war in Asia" (although he signed the SEATO treaty, which committed us to one at the drop of a hat), opposed the military-industrial complex (while surrounding himself with wall-to-wall businessmen), and, one gathers, never really intended to use those Cuban troops we'd been drilling so urgently and rigorously (in fact, Ike pressed the invasion plan warmly on Jack on the very day Jack was inaugurated).

Without wishing to malign that superb survivor,* it seems that whenever Eisenhower could dodge the blame for something, he did so, even if it did later land on young Jack; and whenever he couldn't, he somehow let it be known that he'd had a hunch all along that it had been a mistake. Thus his notorious appearance on a platform with Senator Joe McCarthy, after the latter had accused Ike's patron George C. Marshall of being a traitor, was a "terrible mistake." Ike knew it in his bones all along. And as for his willingness to fly a U-2 reconnaisance over Russia even on May 1 (the equivalent of their doing the same to us on a July 4)—why, that flew in the face of all his retrospective hunches put together. And so on.

It may perhaps be appropriate that this most blameless of presidents should also have permitted unprecedented scope to that most unaccountable of organizations, the CIA. Thus it was under Ike—but not *quite* under Ike—that the CIA "destabilized" Guatemala, to its later distress, and engineered the overthrow of Mossadegh in Iran and the return of the Shah, with results that we're still living with. And it was under Ike, in that same weirdly semi-responsible sense, † that the CIA rigged up the Bay of Pigs operation and handed it over, fully formed, to JFK.

Later, Jack would accept the blame, which never seemed to land on Ike, for the ensuing fiasco—which also turned out to be good politics for *him* (we are a strange people) at the time, but has not helped his historical self much since. But it was hard to see what else he could have done with the quasi-Eisenhower plan. The Cuban exiles were going to be a

---

*Anyone who could keep the U.S. and Britain fighting side by side long enough to end World War II can be excused an awful lot of other things.

†To some degree, the intelligence community tried to reduce *all* our presidents to this condition, most outrageously in the case of Ronald Reagan. So it is possible that Ike was not apprised of all these CIA pranks, any more than either Ike or Jack had to know about their Halloween attempts to undermine Castro. What is certain is that Ike increased the CIA budget way beyond what President Truman had envisaged, and seems to have given Allen Dulles carte blanche to spend it in any way his fancy, or his subordinates', took him.

Prime Minister Macmillan of Great Britain, here meeting JFK for the first time, struck a special bond with the president. "Super Mac," the wise old man of Tory politics, had much to offer the younger man.

JFK, already dressed for a reception, studies the guest list. Gift baskets are waiting to be distributed.

handful by now whether they fought or didn't fight—and whether they lost or won. Enough of them were former followers of Batista, the hated dictator, to ensure a bloody reception even if they did land successfully. Castro and his men were still fresh from beating this same crowd to smithereens, and Fidel was by now at the pinnacle of his local popularity: so it would have required a good deal more from us than a little air cover to overthrow him and make his country swallow another Batista-like regime—if that's even what we wanted.

Whether Castro planned it that way or not, letting the exiles come here in the first place was far and away his most successful political thrust against America. Hell-bent on returning to Cuba by fair means or foul, the exiles have shown their new hosts no peace from that day to this. (As Joan Didion's fine book *Miami* reports, they are still at it, busily destabilizing the most important city on the Florida peninsula.) The CIA merely put icing on the cake by training these zealots in modern combat: after that they were not only itching to fight everyone in sight, they also knew how, though probably not enough to beat Castro. So calling off the Bay of Pigs at that point might have thrown them into a subversive frenzy, while making it succeed was quite possibly beyond our reasonable powers. So the weak third choice of letting the invasion take its chances without us was finally adopted: not a triumph, to be sure, but not quite the young man's folly that it's been painted.

The U-2 incident was another piece of Ike's legacy that would devil Kennedy, though in a more roundabout way. Prior to the episode, Khrushchev had stuck his neck out a dangerous distance to improve relations with the West, banging his shoe on the U.N. table at one moment, to be sure, but visiting Disneyland at the next, in a dazzling display of opéra bouffe. And even as the Russians were stalking our plane, plans were being completed for a summit conference in Paris a few weeks later, which promised the greatest thaw in the Cold War yet—perhaps, we dared hope, an irreversible thaw.

Anyway, we'll never know. Eisenhower blew the summit sky-high with his I-knew-it-all-along decision to unleash the U-2 that day and his subsequent lies about it, and Khrushchev suddenly found himself with no more neck to stick out. Ike's successor was thus practically guaranteed a belligerent Khrushchev, as Nikita struggled to regain ground with his own hard-liners by sticking his tongue out at the first American who walked in the door. And this he virtually did when he met Jack in Vienna only a little more than a year after the U-2 disaster.

The meeting seems to have kicked off with a dialectical browbeating of the old school, the kind you used to hear on street corners, only more so, and quite demeaning as between one world leader and another, and ended in total intransigence. Jack, unfortunately, had made the mistake of arriving at the summit with no demands of his own to speak of, except that the Russians keep their hands off Laos (which they later did), while Nikita walked in with a big one: he wanted, in effect, the whole of Berlin, although Westerners might still be allowed some limited access to their own zone. This breathtaking proposal must be what Kennedy had in mind when he described the Russian negotiating style as "what's mine is mine, what's yours we can negotiate."

No transcripts can convey the sheer "heaviness" of such a man as Khrushchev, and after two days of it Jack seemed quite depressed and shaken by his first encounter with the seemingly, or schemingly, irrational. After a tongue-tied beginning, he had apparently held his own in the more lucid exchanges; but much of what the Russian said was willfully unanswerable. In fact, Jack must have felt as if he'd run into Papa Karamazov and his son Ivan in the same Turkish bath.

"It's going to be a cold winter" were Jack's parting words, and observers say they had never seen him so beaten down or discouraged. But English diplomats who'd been there before advised him against taking it all too seriously and Kennedy began to bounce back soon enough. He had arrived in Vienna primed with good advice vis-à-vis the Russians from General de Gaulle, which still stood up after the bluster had cleared; and after he left, he went on to London and met Harold Macmillan, whose famous coolness must have made a soothing contrast to the mad bear's maulings. In fact, he and "Unflappable Mac" would soon strike up a fast friendship, and this along

with Jack's more measured one with de Gaulle*
were priceless trophies to bring back from his
first Grand Tour. Whatever the fate of Berlin,
the Western Alliance was never stronger in
spirit, as opposed to on paper, than it was in
the Kennedy years.

Khrushchev was to make two sharp follow-
up thrusts at Kennedy's willingness to fight or
lack of it—one in his own sphere and one in
ours. In a sense it might be said that Nikita
won the first one, with his Berlin Wall, and
lost the second, in Cuba. It all depends. If
one bears in mind Khrushchev's bully-boy demands in Vienna, the Wall must have seemed
quite a comedown. Kennedy's main concern
had been the integrity of West Berlin, so he
must have been relieved to settle for a mere
wall on the edge of it ("the lesser of two evils"
he called it). But if one considers the possibility that all Khrushchev realistically hoped
for in the first place was his precious wall,
something to show the boys back home, then
the honors go to him by a whisker. Although
he later quietly dropped his other Viennese
demands, the world had seen his masonry go
up in the passive presence of American tanks.
Who knows, it just might have saved his job
for the moment.

Debate still rages, especially in William F.

*As a measure of how much Jack must have impressed the unimpressable
de Gaulle, it is piquant to note that, a few years later, *Le Grand Charles*
would enter the separatist province of Quebec with the words "*Je suis
québecois*"—a faithful replica of "*Ich bin ein Berliner.*" For the Anglo-
Americo–phobe de Gaulle to have borrowed *any* American's style, for
even a moment, is a compliment for which words simply do not exist
("*n'existent pas*").

*JFK at the desk in the Oval Office emphasizes a
point to a visitor in typical Kennedy fashion.*

The 1960 election, though close in the presidential race, ushered in Democratic majorities in both houses. The president met with House and Senate leaders at regular breakfast meetings. In addition to Senate majority leader Mike Mansfield (right), this breakfast was also attended by Speaker of the House Sam Rayburn, House majority leader John McCormack, and Vice President Johnson.

Buckley's jolly spy novels, about whether and what the U.S. should have done about the Wall before it became a dreary fact of life, like the Eiffel Tower. No doubt a statesman in the nuclear age should in theory continue to play the game of bluff and counter-bluff in every situation—else he concedes every other situation too. But two assumptions about this particular round of the game still seem the most reasonable: (1) that Khrushchev's bluff *probably* could have been called, but (2) that Kennedy didn't think it was worth taking any chances at all over a mere wall. A nuclear war over the city of West Berlin itself would be

hard enough to explain to whatever Americans were still around to ask about it. But a wall? Only a thriller writer would take the risk.

As described earlier, Kennedy saved some face in the NATO countries with his famous wall speech. But he hadn't saved it yet with Khrushchev, or with his own right wing. And many nervous Europeans needed a bit more than a graceful speech to convince them that Kennedy would indeed fight for them in any circumstances at all.

In other words, he needed a show of strength somewhere, and it had to be a little more substantial than an invasion of Grenada, or

Gerald Ford's revenge of the *Mayaguez*. Revisionists since then, most notably Garry Wills, have suggested that Kennedy overreacted badly to the upcoming Cuban Missile Crisis, which needn't have been a crisis at all: all we had to do was unobtrusively remove *our* missiles from Turkey, which we'd been planning to do anyway, and presto! no crisis.

But Wills is an intensely domestic historian, and foreign countries hardly enter his work at all, or, presumably, his calculations. Globally speaking, this was the one moment we could *not* remove the bases from Turkey. One more apparent concession from us to Russia and Kennedy's credibility as a Western leader was gone forever. Americans, mesmerized since that time by Red Guards and student protests, have forgotten the extent to which postwar Europe looked to us for tangible signs of strength; and up to now, Kennedy, so far from seeming trigger-happy, had shown the world no real muscle at all, either at the iniquitous Bay or over Berlin.

Now Khrushchev was serving him up a fast pitch in his own ballpark, which, if met with decisively enough, could make up for all that in one stroke. By ostentatiously planting his missiles in Cuba, the Soviet leader was attempting a bluff which Jack felt could, this time, safely be called. Kennedy knew his man by now, and he moved forward with the kind of assurance his opponent could only pretend to feel, in his overextended position. To be sure, the night that Kennedy ordered the Russian missiles out, my friends and I raced off frantically to confession, several of us for the first time in years: *we* didn't know we were

safe. But Jack had received signals from Nikita, both between sessions in Vienna and in the form of personal gifts afterward, that Khrushchev had to go through these hostile motions to appease his own hard-liners—but please don't take it personally. And Jack may have felt it a good bet that nobody goes to nuclear war in that mood: still wanting to be liked.

Anyway, our jubilation and everyone else's, when the Russians sheepishly picked up their missiles and sailed away, was intense beyond recapturing. The bully of Vienna had received his comeuppance, all scores were settled, and it should be a long time indeed before anyone else decided to test Jack Kennedy's strength again—at least in this hemisphere.* Later Khrushchev would talk of Kennedy with rare affection and respect, and perhaps partly out of these very things would sign the Nuclear Test Ban Treaty on August 6, 1963, fulfilling Jack's fondest dream just before he died: a satisfactory outcome, one might say, to their man-on-bear confrontations.

This set of circumstances is worth holding in mind, because it has since been suggested by a certain revisionist that Jack at this point was still smarting from both the Bay of Pigs and the humiliations of Vienna and that his machismo still demanded more blood. So, of course, he *had* to escalate in Vietnam.

To which I can only say that this is the kind of theory that people can form about you only

*Dean Rusk has since informed us that Jack did indeed have a back-up plan to throw the Cuban-Turkish missile exchange question into the U.N. for arbitration: so Khrushchev's capitulation to his bluff must have tasted all the sweeter and done everything for Jack's confidence that it could possibly have needed.

when you've been away for a while, and they are free to reconstruct you any way they like. Nobody who was familiar with the Jack of the press conferences and the cool speeches ever dreamed in his or her wildest moments that the man was still nursing some psychic wound or another, or even a dueling scar from old Vienna. His manner before Khrushchev and after seemed exactly the same to me. For instance, someone who saw him shortly after the missile crisis was taken aback to see him, feet on desk, puffing happily on a Cuban cigar. "There is only so much a man can do for his country," explained the contented president. Now, say what you will about such a roguish fellow, it remains my firm belief that he doesn't exactly need a war.

It probably makes more sense to view Jack's involvement in Vietnam first of all in terms of our SEATO commitments there and of President Eisenhower's famous letter to President Diem, personally pledging support for Diem's own government. This letter had since attained virtual treaty status, because neighboring countries had, in Schlesinger's words, "staked their own security on it," thus turning themselves into the dominoes that were needed to fulfill the Domino Theory.

It could be argued today that Kennedy should simply have abrogated both the treaty and the letter before things got hopelessly out of hand.

But the sanctity of agreements was much on Jack's mind at the moment. His most urgent interest around then was his nuclear test–ban treaty, and the biggest stumbling block between him and it was the general understanding that the Russians used such treaties strictly to tie *your* hands, not theirs.

And then there were the NATO and ANZUS* allies to consider. Over here in Fortress America we tend to think about our wars as if they all began and ended with nothing in mind but American votes. But Kennedy of all presidents knew that other countries had people in them too, and that some of them at least took our mutual defense treaties a lot more seriously than we did, as simple matters of life and death. And if we were even thinking about retiring our famous nuclear umbrella any day soon, we had better make sure those treaties held up every link, down to the weakest, down even to the Eisenhower letter to Diem.

Otherwise our allies might say, If you can tear up one piece of paper, why not two? or three? We could protest all day that Europe and the Antipodes were different and that NATO and ANZUS were the serious treaties,

---

*Australia and New Zealand barely registered on our consciousness at the time, but it was they who naturally felt the most concern about disorder in Southeat Asia, and the Australians in particular, who contributed the most troops besides ourselves to the Vietnam War.

Night after night the president, especially in the early days of his administration when there were no social functions, worked until the wee hours alone in his office. He read the mail and would dictate his replies into an old-fashioned Dictaphone.

but the ANZUS countries flatly wouldn't believe it, and the NATO ones might at least start looking around for other security arrangements.

Since retiring the umbrella remained Kennedy's first order of business, it followed that *something* had to be done about the SEATO countries, all thirteen thousand miles away of them, and about the unworkable arrangement in Vietnam, whereby we had not only pledged to defend one half of a country against its recently separated other but also against itself if it threatened one man, Diem.

Kennedy's first challenge down and out in Southeast Asia blessedly occurred in the relative privacy of a turbulent backwater named Laos—which is pretty much like exploding your H-bombs in the desert. But even there he did not really satisfy anyone, because of his deep-down reluctance to send American combat troops over there. He zigged and he zagged on this, to the point where it was quite possible to accuse him of belligerence and weakness on alternate days: but he was merely writhing in the old Truman straitjacket. And meanwhile the Russians too were doing a little something down there and *not* doing it at the same time, in the grim, ungainly dance of the Cold Warriors.

The basic trouble with the Doctrine was

Unless absorbed in correspondence or facing visitors, the president rarely sat at his desk. He would roam, glance at television, scan the newspapers, look in on Evelyn Lincoln, his secretary. Here he leans over the desk behind him, where stacks of newspapers, magazines, and documents were kept.

that it contained no instructions as to *how* we were going to protect all those countries. The public wanted displays of strength all right, but at absolutely no risk to American life; the wilder elements (and they were no tiny minority) would probably have preferred the total nuking of great world cities to the death of one American soldier. Such was the mood of the fifties.

Later, cooler generations have taken Kennedy to task for his apparent obsession with limited, brush-fire wars of counter-insurgency waged by special CIA-trained forces—but consider the alternative. For years now the country had lived without blinking under the concept of Massive Retaliation, with all the unthinkable slaughter it implied; and conservatives even talked seriously of H-bombing the Chinese before they could build a bomb of their own: Massive Preemption, if you like. In fact, it would be instructive, in a morbid sort of way, to list the number of times, from Korea on down, that nuclear warfare had been passionately advocated—and not just by lion-hearted editorial writers but by bona-fide presidential advisers, most notably including the Joint Chiefs of Staff, whose voices should be kept in mind constantly roaring in the background, mostly for "more," throughout the whole period.

Nothing the supposedly aggressive Kennedy ever did to the world was one-tenth as violent as the advice he received about it. In such a heady, sword-clanking atmosphere, even his more extraneous interventions (such as the one in the Congo) must surely be seen as resolute attempts to scale things down, from the great Massive Retaliation pipedream. Of course he had to act tough about it: when you are diminishing a nation's image of itself, you had better act tough. But his tactics otherwise make perfectly good sense, without resort to words like "obsession." The public and the Doctrine both wanted certain lines held, and they had to be held by *something*: hence special forces, green berets, and the like—the p and the D didn't really much care what you used and Kennedy was simply hell-bent on knocking the nuclear alternative out of the realm of discussion forever. Although he himself was deeply committed to negotiation and more negotiation (in Laos, especially, Jack seized on every opening that an absolutely impossible situation could offer him), he also knew that

The Third World and the struggle for independence had been a prime concern of Senator Kennedy. African leaders had often visited him in room 362 of the Senate Office Building. His speech on the need for Algerian independence had energized these exiled leaders. Now, as president, he was in a position to carry out his firm conviction that the African continent should not be allowed to become yet another Cold War zone.

diplomacy without visible power is as weak as the U.N.; and meanwhile the "enemy," appearing in different faces everywhere, seemed to be probing at us and calling our bluster more and more confidently each day: were we *afraid* to send troops or what? And what about our famous air cover that never shows up? Were we even worth worrying about at this point?

Critics have since said that the Bay of Pigs made Kennedy even more belligerent, but insider evidence all runs the other way: the Bay had made him much more skeptical of both the military and the CIA, with their grandiose view of the outside world as alternately our plaything and our experimental lab. At the same time he still had to act on the only information he could get and this still inevitably came from the CIA and the military, and the information was telling him with virtually one voice now that the Vietnam domino, which was already leaning on the Laos domino, had reached its own crisis point and could easily be lost if we didn't intervene and in force. And of course the world watched: NATO, SEATO, and all the little dominoes everywhere.

Under any circumstances, it would have been a ridiculous war for us—so much so, in fact, that even in *these* circumstances hawks

On February 13, 1961, United Nations Ambassador Adlai Stevenson called to report that former premier Patrice Lumumba of the Democratic Republic of the Congo (now Zaïre) had been assassinated. The news Kennedy finally received at the moment this photograph was taken was already a month old. Lumumba in fact had been murdered before Kennedy's inauguration.

139

soon began defending it simply on the grounds that we were there already. It was the very quintessence of both quiet and ugly Americanism in its airy suppositions that our conscript army, fighting in totally alien terrain, could succeed where French veterans, who knew the ground and had something at stake, had failed; and further that we would somehow prove more *popular* than the French, in a land that had made it crystal clear that no Westerners *whatever* need apply.

To make matters slightly worse, especially for our first Catholic president, there lurked within the regular war a nasty little religious one between Catholics and Buddhists, and our man Diem and even more so his brother General Nhu turned out to be not only Catholics but fanatical bigots about it to boot. In fact, a case could be made that Diem himself abrogated any further right to our support by breaking a hard-won promise we'd extracted from him to leave the Buddhists alone, by launching a bloody assault on Buddhist pagodas even as he was supposed to be concentrating his energies on the Vietcong enemy.

Everyone remembers the picture of the monk incinerating himself in protest in the middle of Saigon: it was probably the second most famous photo to come out of that flaming, napalm-saturated war (the first being that of the little girl, also on fire, running, screaming in pain and fear, toward the camera). Many Americans probably began to think seriously about the war for the first time around then,

and, if so, their first thoughts must have been confused ones. Our assistance so far (and such as it was) had been based precisely on our pledge to Diem, yet we couldn't continue honorably to provide it, let alone hope to win with it, so long as Diem remained in charge.

To top off the nightmare, for first Catholic presidents in particular, was our very own Francis Cardinal Spellman, who had lately developed grotesque delusions of world statesmanship, and seemed to have constituted himself some sort of American patron to Diem and the Nhus (both General and Madame). This kind of thing had been more or less okay so long as the Terrible Three were all fighting the Communists—Church and State were accustomed to winking at each other over the Red Menace—but decidedly not when they were persecuting Buddhists. Kennedy of all people could not afford to overlook a potential marriage of American right-wing Catholic sentiment with wanton local barbarism; yet he also couldn't very well cancel our obligations overnight because of it.

Around this time, Henry Cabot Lodge, our current man on the spot, seems to have decided, along with the inevitable CIA, that the perfect solution to the whole Diem problem was simply to let the man be assassinated (there were always plenty of volunteers), and for years people assumed that this decision emanated from Jack himself: but later accounts indicate that he was furious about it—and for good reason. Suddenly any prospects he might have

JFK and Bobby conferring in the East Room.

had for ending the war soon were sharply fore-closed. We couldn't very well have a man killed just to give ourselves an excuse to leave his country: we would now have to wait for America to become exasperated with a whole new regime. But well before anything like that could happen, Jack was dead himself, murdered almost one month to the day after Diem, taking his long-range plans with him.

It is ironical that so much of the posthumous sniping at Jack's Vietnamese policy should have come from doves rather than his natural critics, the hawks. It is indeed true that he failed to wind down the war, but it is equally true, and surely more significant that, despite the din emanating from the Joint Chiefs and other well-wishers, he never let it get off the ground, either, and nothing about him suggests to me that he ever would have.

Jack's overall record was, as we have seen, surprisingly unaggressive, to the point where perhaps only a war hero could have gotten away with it. His predecessor had sent troops to Lebanon and his successor would send them to the Dominican Republic, but Jack just scratched away with his covert operations, never coming close to invoking U.S. war powers. The Cuban refugees in Miami recognized bitterly that, fine words to the contrary, he was never going to commit American forces to their beloved reconquest, and we have also seen how he was quite willing to lose a little face over the Berlin Wall to avoid even the

remotest chance of a nuclear war. In fact, the only real risk he took in the Cuban Missile Crisis turns out to have been less a risk with every new piece of information. There really are moments in life when it is quite safe for the matador to kneel down in front of the bull—especially when the matador has a back-up plan in his pocket.

Translating all this to Vietnam: would the restless Jack have sat still for an endless bloody war, even when it began to tear his own nation apart in 1965? Would the cautious Jack actually have thrown this quality to the winds long enough to use nuclear bombs on the North instead? Or, finally, were the global stakes ever high enough to throw even as much as we eventually did into this small, distant, disconnected land? All that we know for sure is that Jack increased the number of our advisers over there from two thousand to sixteen thousand, which is still quite some difference from the war we wound up getting. The Gulf of Tonkin declaration had been neither concocted nor extorted, and in fact, within the conventions of Cold War usage, it was still possible not to call it a war at all, but a paramilitary containment operation (yes, that's how we talked).

Still, I suppose he left the situation slightly more insoluble, if that be possible, than he found it, for which his only excuse could possibly be that he didn't know he was going to leave it so soon. What is particularly puzzling

---

about it is that Jack himself had talked against such futile involvements as this many times, not least in his famous Free Algeria speech. And in his first talks with de Gaulle, in the spring of 1961, he had actually wondered out loud whether the suppressed antipathy between Russia and China would ever come to the full boil so long as there were any sort of Westerners around. So it seems he had long since abandoned the idea that communism was a monolith, but still felt he had to live for a while with its consequences. China and North Vietnam, the duo we seemed to dread the most, were in reality ancient enemies, and the only thing that could bring them together was us. But, unfortunately, we seemed treaty-bound to do just that.

Beyond all this is the fact that Jack just plain stalled. He indeed "never feared to negotiate," and was actually about to enter negotiations with Castro himself when he died. But he was fearful about committing American troops, and he was, let's face it, fearful of endangering his prized second term by losing yet another country to the Communists—a country whose importance had been insanely exaggerated just by our being there.

Schlesinger has called Vietnam Kennedy's "worst mistake," and it certainly turned out to be, as it gradually swelled into Johnson's mistake and then Nixon's mistake. And yet, and yet—considering the difficulty his successors had in ending the war with even a facsimile of honor, perhaps Kennedy did need that second term to do it decently himself. The nation in 1963 was not particularly anti-war yet: the mood varied from indifferent to hawkish, and I remember the liberal editor of the magazine where I worked arguing with me over a peace letter I had signed as late as 1964. Surely, he said, we had to live up to our obligations.

So perhaps Kennedy did have to take on an outright hawk like Goldwater and beat him before he could take his case successfully to the nation, and to a Kennedy Congress. If so, his worst mistake becomes once more what it was in the first place: namely, driving through the streets of Dallas in an open-topped car on November 22, 1963.

Still, the war began to hurt his reputation from the first moment that LBJ escalated it. Americans tend to see only one foreign country at a time, and so long as that infernal war raged (and much longer), no one seemed to remember anything else that Kennedy, or Johnson, or even, to a lesser extent, Nixon, had done. And yet if you travel much in the

TOP: *During the steel crisis Kennedy confers with AFL-CIO chief George Meany and Secretary of Labor Arthur Goldberg.*

BOTTOM: *Kennedy meets with United Auto Workers president Walter Reuther and Inland Steel chairman Joseph Block, whose company had refused to raise prices and thereby forced U.S. Steel and the other steel companies to bring their prices back down.*

Third World, as my colleague M. Lowe has done, you will find people who remember dozens of other things; and you will still see the familiar reassuring face, on the walls of mud huts and modern offices alike, of the president *who gave us hope*, not to mention technical assistance, food, funding, and everything that it was in him to give.

But you don't have to travel that far to find that Kennedy lives. Europeans, who are frequently puzzled by the volatility of our devotions, still hold Jack in the same high if slightly suspended esteem. What *would* he have done next? And in our own country you hear the famous style echoing off every second young Democrat who hopes someday to be president. The unfortunate Gary Hart was an extreme example, but the group known affectionately (and briefly) as the Seven Dwarfs, who tried to pick up Hart's pieces in 1987, each carried at least one aspect of Kennedy as a talisman, like a sprig of heather or a shamrock in the buttonhole. And these people are paid to read the public mind—or, failing that, at least the public polls, which show (according to the Harris Survey of March 1987) that Jack Kennedy still stands an easy first in virtually every category that goes into the popular concept of what a president ought to be.

Unfortunately, there are few more forlorn sights in nature than that of a politician trying to borrow another man's style, and at this writing we have already seen two candidates obliged to leave the room because of bad Kennedy imitations, though of very different kinds (Gary Hart's was really off the wall). But of course all imitations miss the point. Probably the last Democrat to give no thought whatever to Kennedy's style—if only to snarl enviously at it—was Jack himself. Style was simply what was left over from the business of being himself. So the "next Kennedy" will have no choice but to be an original.

Perhaps the essence of how the *original* original blended style and substance into a single, unselfconscious whole is best captured in the speech he gave at American University on June 10, 1963, concerning coexistence in a nuclear world, where "we breathe the same air. We all cherish our children's future. And we are all mortal." This was surely considered a very stylish speech by its English-speaking audience, but this can hardly have been the element that impelled Nikita Khrushchev to call it the greatest speech uttered by an American since Franklin Roosevelt. Style seldom survives translation, especially when Russian verbs are involved, and Nikita was hardly on the lookout for it in this tremulous moment.

The test-ban speech in any language was simply a model of intellectual passion, conveyed with overwhelming persuasiveness, and

The president facing a visitor. He would often stand like this, slightly leaning on the desk, to alleviate his back pain.

as far as Khrushchev was concerned that was probably that. Although the great Diplomatic Machine must be served, and negotiations rumbled on for a bit, the Nuclear Test Ban Treaty was actually signed with unprecedented dispatch—and all, ultimately, on the strength of a single speech.

And that, or even the remote possibility of that, is, I suppose, what one misses most keenly about Jack Kennedy. The kind of man-to-man directness, which politics usually knocks out of you bit by bit, until most diplomatic conversation sounds like robots talking in code, had miraculously survived in these two remarkable men, thus enabling Jack and Nikita to cut a deal on a life-and-death matter like kids in a schoolyard.

Once upon a time, Franklin Roosevelt thought he understood "Uncle Joe" Stalin, which meant that he thought he could manipulate him: which in turn meant that *somebody* was going to get manipulated around here. Kennedy's understandings on the other hand were just that, and not simply an endless series of wrestling holds. He even remembered the things you learn about people *before* you go into politics, and so knew how to locate the man buried inside the politician and how to salute him like a fellow human and not just

as a fellow cardsharp. And if this sounds fanciful, how else does one explain the numbers of foreign statesmen who genuinely seemed to *like* him in a manner quite unlike the run of political friendships, a manner so obviously promising for world peace?

And then there was his concentration. A lady of no particular importance or nubility who chanced to find herself Jack Kennedy's dinner partner one night later reported that his attention to her had been total throughout, as if she had been the test-ban treaty itself; and of course Pablo Casals said the same about Jack and music. *Nothing* came between him and the object at hand. And no obfuscation of language could keep him from seeing it and saying it straight.

In the current Tower of Babel that is Official Washington (it was just a molehill in Jack's day), no gift of his would be more useful right now than this last one: the ability to cut the cackle, be it oral or typed in triplicate, down to the unchanging human essences. But you can't just ask a candidate to send out for these qualities; all you can do perhaps is to ask the voters and other king-makers to send out for another kind of candidate.

Beware of *imitations*, though. Real Kennedys imitate no one.

The president needed eyeglasses from time to time, and when working, he would push them up on his forehead. In time, he became sensitive to the need for glasses, and this photographer, unaware of this, got into trouble while preparing a major magazine cover showing the glasses.

FIVE

Bobby and Jack

And then it was all over: the light went out on the Kennedy pageant like a stage light. A strange piece of Cold War flotsam named Lee Harvey Oswald, whose motives have not been fully pinned down to this day, equipped only with a mail-order gun and maybe a colleague someplace up the road, contrived to shatter that galvanic brain and plunge the whole room in darkness. The good dream was over, and we'd just have to go back to the way we were before.

The unique impact of Jack Kennedy's assassination can still be nicely gauged by the number of people who remember exactly what they were doing at the time. In my lifetime, Pearl Harbor is the only other event to have commandeered, so imperiously, the nation's wandering memory cells. V-E Day, V-J Day, Roosevelt's death—we probably remember something about all of them; but exactly where we were sitting, or what sandwich we were

Bobby Kennedy's appointment to the cabinet had not been a smooth one. He himself had resisted such an exposed position amidst the near-universal cries of "nepotism." But Jack insisted and in retrospect it turned out to be an inspired choice, in spite of Jack's aside to him: "Don't smile too much or they'll think we are happy about the appointment." Here he is in his office in early 1961.

Attorney General Bobby Kennedy, here at his home in McLean, Virginia, with his daughter Mary Courtney (left) and pursued by his wife, Ethel, during a football game (above), also has become a style setter. His private seminars involving American and foreign scholars and experts in all areas of science and philosophy have begun to make a major contribution to the search for solutions to the problems of the sixties, both at home and abroad.

In 1956, young Bobby Kennedy was appointed majority counsel of the Senate Select Committee on Improper Activities in the Labor and Management Field, better known as the McClellan Committee, where his relentless pursuit of labor racketeers and their management allies earned him the ruthless image which was to plague him all of his political life.

eating (tuna on toast in my case)—that kind of poignantly pointless detail remains strictly reserved for November 22, 1963.

The feeling is hard to reassemble, because alongside our incredible personal loss, we also felt in a more abstract sense that "they just can't do this" to an American president, any American president—and if they can, what's to become of us? So there was, mixed with our grief, an element of Pearl Harbor too, of shock attack: a premonition that some kind of international chaos was on its way, or possibly here already.

Other presidents have been shot at, and some have been killed, but of these only Abraham Lincoln seems to have elicited anything like the sense of desolation and abandonment that Jack called forth, and that in only parts of the country. Lincoln, to his believers, was simply the only man who could have made the Union work again; hopes in Kennedy were naturally vaguer and smaller, but perhaps more plentiful. America's world had become vastly more variegated since Lincoln's day, and Kennedy seemed to offer at least some hope in every corner of it.

Thus along with grief and outrage came a queasy apprehension for the future—apprehension which has since been handsomely borne out by events. A death in the prime of a great life is as cruel as it is tantalizing: Martin Luther King's greatest work was already behind him when he died, with blacks starting to turn on their own to other leaders at the time of his murder, while Bobby was still hovering on a most uncertain threshold of public acceptance in his last days. But Jack was *there*, and his best work lay right there in front of him.

By dying at that time and in that way, Kennedy was fated to leave us with an infinite series of question marks, some trivial and some heartbreaking. On the lighter side, I can hardly have been the only one to have predicted that day, with a sarcasm born of newspaper reading, that *someone* would be arrested by sundown, and that the someone would be sandy-haired and of medium height, and, to suit the specifics of this case, neither a Negro nor a Communist nor preferably a Texan or militant right-winger. Assassinations have to be cleaned up in a hurry, to keep panic at bay, and ideally the suspect's identity should not set off further explosions, either at home or abroad. As it turned out, Lee Harvey Oswald was considerably more complicated than we were told right then, but at the time he seemed an inspired choice, one in a million, and almost too good to be true; and when he was promptly snuffed the next day, before he had time to utter a word, by the equally neutral Jack Ruby, it seemed like the slickest, most thorough cleanup imaginable.

But there is a price to be paid for such slickness, and we have paid for it in the form of a thousand and one theories about what really happened that day, each more tedious than the last. When the Warren Commission report came out, itself a bit too hastily, its defenders claimed immediately that if the official version were *not* true, Attorney General Robert Kennedy would surely go to any lengths to track down the real killer. But Bobby's mute acceptance of the report did not deter a gathering slew of writers who seemed even more eager for justice than Bobby himself. The net result of their efforts, despite some honorable work, was to turn Jack's death into something of a yellow-press oddity, on the lines of *Garbo Speaks*, or that venerable standby *Did Roosevelt Really Die?* Perhaps Bobby (who moves front stage now) foresaw all that, and decided not to add one more word to it. After all, suppose an investigation had led to Cuba, or even to the Cuban exiles in Miami—what then? Supposing, God forfend, it had led to Russia?

From now on, our closest clue to "what Jack would have done" in this and that case has to be Bobby himself, the chosen disciple, and the brother to whom Jack had confided his views on world affairs so long ago when they were both still young, and presumably in all the years since. In this light, Bobby's silence on the assassination takes on more telling possibilities. "Would we want to go to war over this?" one can imagine Jack saying to him more than once. Would it be good for the nation, the world?

Bobby was always supposed to be the *really* tough Kennedy, the one with blood in his eye. But he had worked at Jack's side so long, and knew his mind so well, that by now he was probably able to follow Jack's instincts as easily as his own. And if one can imagine the depth of his personal loss, one can also see how he

Bobby Kennedy at his desk at Justice.

might want to follow Jack's instincts right now. "Let us put all that behind us and move forward," one can almost hear *either* brother saying; and the instruction covers a lot of ground, including Bobby's own past and future. So long as Jack was still around, Bobby's tough-guy persona complemented his brother's urbanity nicely; with Bobby snapping and snarling at his heels, Jack never had to act tough himself. Bobby *was* his fist, and his Irish temper too. But now there was no place further for that act to go.

Not that I believe Bobby's subsequent mellowing was the result of calculation. It seems more likely that Jack's death simply wrung the cockiness out of him like blood from a sponge,

and after that he lost some of the taste for it (not that it wasn't still in there ticking like a time bomb). Another factor might be mentioned here, although it seems quaintly old-fashioned to say it about anybody these days; but Bobby really was, or at least tried his damnedest to be, a good Catholic, and for such a one real grief is supposed to run much deeper than vengeance. Never mind about not getting mad, getting even, etc., and all the other Kennedy battle cries: those were rules for the contests of life, not rules of the heart. Grief for a religious man is major, a tragic acting out of love on an empty stage: vengeance is tactics, and even its sweetness is overrated. (It usually tastes rotten.)

Bobby knew in his feisty soul that the best thing he could do for Jack now was not to waste years tracing putative killers to the corners of the globe, but to spend those years faithfully and "with vigor" executing the Legacy as best he understood it, and even as he embodied it. And for Bobby, far and away the most important part of the Legacy—in fact the part he may have put there himself—was compassion, and this must have comported well with his sorrowing mood of the next few months and years. At any rate, he seemed during that time to take on another dimension, a sort of adult melancholy, if you will, and a quiet determination to make the most of what was left to him.

While Bobby grieved in his way, the public grieved in its: which in this case meant, among other things, running out and naming everything in sight after Jack, from Idlewild Airport to Cape Canaveral, to God knows how many streets, boulevards, and high schools across the land. It was as if we wanted to be reminded of him constantly and forever.

Yet even then, signs of our fickleness were bubbling near the surface, which is their natural home. The National Football league kicked off, so to speak, by playing its full schedule of games two days after the assassination on the grounds that "Jack would have wanted it"— as if one's decision to honor or not honor a fallen hero were up to *him*, let alone his imaginary wishes.

Still, our grief "held" in its fashion, long enough at least for LBJ to win that landslide, even though his opponent Barry Goldwater had actually been a closer friend of Jack's. And there would be other memory surges. For instance, when we actually did put a man on the moon, within the decade, as Kennedy had promised, it was as if one of his pleasantest dreams had come true from the grave. In fact, throughout that whole season of astronautical wonders, his memory shone as bright as ever; and despite the troubling questions being asked more and more about how we got into Vietnam in the first place, even yippies were heard to invoke the spirit of Jack Kennedy as if he were somehow one of them after all. Meanwhile, in the somewhat slower world of Democratic Party politics, his last name is still, in 1988, assumed by some to be electoral magic, and even today a few keepers of the flame continue to press his luckless brother Teddy to run for president, as if in deference to Joseph P.'s strange belief that any son of his would do.

Yet perhaps our mourning for Jack was, like so many things we pick up eagerly and put down again like Christmas toys, "too hot not to cool down" from the very start. When his name was taken *off* his pet Cape Canaveral, it was as if a sober nation were trying to rectify its excesses of the night before. Did we really sit vigil by our TV sets for two solid days until the last mourner had trailed past the coffin in the Capitol rotunda? And did the floodgates open again like dams when Jackie laid her wreath at Arlington? How strange it all seems. Our feelings change so fast that it's small wonder that our national memory is correspondingly weak. Nothing, even despair, lodges long enough.

Thus cooled off, we may find it a little easier to accept certain diminishments of the legend, both of the politician and the man. The first, or strictly political, revision of Kennedy was probably inevitable, in view of all those question marks and unfinished political sentences in his career, and because a certain seesawing of reputation is a necessary part of the work of history.

But personal revisionism is another matter. It is, if anything, not the work but the play of history—but usually it isn't history at all, but gossip, imagination, and a distillation of million-dollar memoirs written by assistant gardeners. Unfortunately for Jack, his favorite, and perhaps only, vice was the one we most like to read about: and so we come inevitably and with unwonted reluctance to the subject of women.

It is not for me to gauge the strength or relative resistibility of another man's temptations, but it should be said right off that Jack's must have been formidable. There seems to be no doubt by now that Joseph P. Kennedy taught all his boys, by example if not outright precept, a rather freewheeling, me-Tarzan approach to sex; and granted the singular popularity of the subject, one can well see even the most independent of sons being prepared to go along with his old man on that one.

Thus Jack lacked some of the checks and balances that are needed, working around the clock, to keep most young people on the rails. Instead, and positively fortified with a father's blessing, our young hero soon found himself launched upon an ocean of opportunity too staggering to contemplate. As he was a handsome, charming, articulate young millionaire, it is only surprising that he wasn't promptly drowned under a weight of assorted scandals, financial claims, and paternity suits like a regular millionaire, or that he ever became a serious man at all.

And entry into politics can only have made things worse. It is sometimes said in Washington that the only woman a politician cannot impress (and blessed be the exceptions) is his own wife; and politicians must impress or die. Lecturing, it seems, can be a special torment, because the "high" of holding an audience and moving it at your bidding can be followed by a mischievous emptiness, which craves another kind of high—and Jack didn't enjoy either drugs or drinking, the usual alternatives for performers. If by chance you also happen to be a *star* politician, as Jack was from the start, you can probably also convince yourself that you are doing the other party a favor anyway, somewhere between signing autographs and bestowing a royal blessing. (Nor is

Although he was only one of eleven cabinet members (U.N. Ambassador Adlai Stevenson had cabinet ranking and so had Postmaster General Edward Day), the fact that he was the president's brother easily catapulted Bobby into the number-two government position, normally reserved for the secretary of state. Here, Dean Rusk is questioned on some points relating to an ambassadorial appointment.

this *just* a question of male condescension: I'm sure that Catherine the Great felt exactly the same way.)

However, a good excuse is still an excuse, so I'll leave it at that. One thing, though, that has always puzzled me about this is how Jack ever managed to square his Don Juanism with his Catholic upbringing, however vestigial that may have been. I can only presume that in the Kennedy family, a father's imprimatur easily overruled a clerical one, but even so, Jack did show faint traces of a religious conscience in his extreme carefulness that no one get hurt along the way (no one did, that I know of), and in his efforts to keep the whole thing as light and "venial" as possible. Ben Bradlee, a practiced reporter and editor who probably saw Jack socially as often as anyone, swears that he never guessed about the other women, and so does my colleague Jacques Lowe, who spent so many other hours with Jack in private.

And finally, there is the vexed question of Kennedy's health, and its possible effects on his other behavior. Ever since the PT boat saga, Jack's injuries had denied him his full share of physical expression, which, I know from personal experience, can be extremely frustrating. But then in 1948, just as Jack was entering politics, his familiar back pain and

Both Kennedys distrusted J. Edgar Hoover. Bobby, especially, who intended to pursue white-collar crime and organized crime figures alike, found Hoover, who had concentrated his efforts on real and imagined Communists and other "enemies of the state," wanting. Bobby tried to bring the FBI, nominally a part of the Justice Department, under control. But Hoover had his own supporters and, for the time being, stayed.

malaria suddenly had to make way for a formidable new member of the family: Addison's disease, an affliction which usually translates to a sentence of death—but which doesn't tell you when. After the last rites of the Church had been administered (themselves like the tolling of some great bell), the first doctor gave Jack perhaps a year to live, and he later gave himself another ten or so, but the sentence was always there.

Congressman Kennedy faded away to a shadow for a while (usually under the public guise of malaria), and only the introduction of cortisone brought him back gradually to presidential size and shape. Herbert Parmet suggests that the cortisone may also have fired up Jack's already ample sex drives; but it could be that the death sentence, and the sense of time running out, fired them up even more. When you've been at death's door, you feel the world owes you one.

Anyhow, this one weakness,* or at least lack of heroic virtue, has been scored very harshly against him, even in our own sloppy times, and I'm afraid one of the reasons for this has to be Chappaquiddick, where, of course, he wasn't even present. Because it was there, in

*The weakness has also been shared by so many great men in the arts and sciences as well as politics that its use as a weapon against any one practitioner is almost invariably capricious. For instance, Lord Palmerston, the popular nineteenth-century prime minister, got away with it for years, while Charles Stewart Parnell, the dangerous Irish radical, slipped just once and was destroyed by it. The weapon is always there, in all periods. Incidentally, I gather that in certain Muslim societies, a leader who did *not* have this weakness would be considered no leader at all.

Bobby's management style was extremely relaxed. He worked in shirtsleeves and often at senior staff meetings a football would be tossed around the cavernous Attorney General's office.

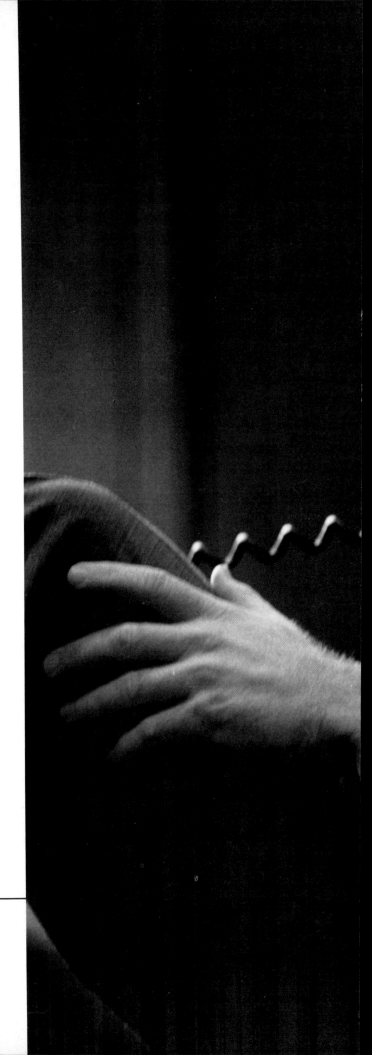

the early dawn of Women's Lib, that we thought we saw for the first time what Kennedys really felt about women. The famous "girls in the boiler room" became transformed in the public imagination from the loyal staff workers they undoubtedly were into some species of ever-ready playmate. And when one of their number, Mary Jo Kopechne, drowned in Teddy's car that night, it seemed to the world as if Teddy and his henchmen had worked just a little bit harder at perfecting his alibi than they did at rescuing Mary Jo: and no number of protestations to the contrary by Teddy ever quite erased this, because they came too late.

In an ordinary family, of course, all this would have been his problem and no one else's. But such was the force of the Kennedy legend that from that night on, I found some people thinking a little less highly of *Jack* as well.

Alas, poor Teddy, perhaps the last and saddest victim of his father's dream. As caretaker of the legislative side of the Legacy, he belongs in our story all right (in fact his role has at times been crucial), yet in any other family in the world, except the Windsors, I doubt if a boy like Teddy would even have dreamed about going into national politics at all. Three such vocations in a family is an awful lot to ask, and I have always had the feeling that what seemed like fun for Jack and Bobby has

been terribly hard, brow-creasing labor for Teddy. For instance, where Jack could talk about things like poverty from the head and Bobby from the heart, Teddy can only talk from the memory, of things other people said first, and the freshness is gone.

Thus the Legacy landed at last and in full murderous force on the brother least designed to handle it. Lacking his brothers' buoyant, revivifying sense of vocation, but weighed down by their monumental legends, it is no wonder that Teddy went AWOL on occasion. And it seems like just part of his luck to wind up having trouble with a nautical rescue of the very kind that had once made Jack famous. And then, as if to complete the parody, he also felt he had to send for his advisers, as if this were some missile crisis or other, before he could even tell the world what happened that night. But in fact, he was merely acting like an average sort of rich kid in a muddle, and not like his brother at all.

It is surely no knock on Teddy to say that he lacked his brothers' prodigious gifts. In some ways he has needed even more character than they in his lion-hearted determination to carry on anyhow and become a highly effective senator, defending his brothers' dreams against a sea of petty, mean-spirited budget cuts, and keeping them politically alive for a less greedy

The Attorney General's office is easily the largest office in Washington, D.C. Yet somehow Bobby managed to make it all human. Crayon drawings by his children lined the walls; his dog, Brumus, often roamed the hall; and Kennedy would eat his lunch of clam chowder, an apple, and a glass of milk at his desk.

generation to rediscover. But why did we ever expect so much of him personally? Unfortunately, perhaps, because he is cursed with a voice which reminds us unfailingly of the other two, and so comparisons are made, to nobody's advantage. (I'm convinced that if the Kennedys talked like other people, even like most other New Englanders, the Family Legend and our godlike expectations of it would shrink to manageable size overnight.)

For some years, and in the teeth of every disappointment, friends of the family continued to hope that Teddy somehow embodied the legend anyway. But Teddy himself ended this wistful game abruptly if inadvertently in 1979 when, in answer to a Roger Mudd question, he couldn't think of a single reason he wanted to be president. This was not denseness* on his part; obviously the man just doesn't want to be president. Even among Kennedys this must sometimes happen. This admission must have made it clearer to everybody that the Kennedy Legacy is not embodied in *anybody*, but is a treasury of actions and attitudes available to all, and that right now it depends for its life not on finding yet more Kennedys but on learning what we can from the ones we had.

The last true claimant was, of course, Bobby—and not on a basis of blood alone. Bobby had already made it on his own as a truly terrifying prosecutor for the McClellan Labor and Management Committee. Much of the myth of Kennedy belligerence dates back to Bobby's celebrated assaults on Jimmy Hoffa and the Mafia, the former of which assaults had a ring of personal vendetta to it, right down to the fabled glaring matches between the two men, and it almost tempted some tender-hearted citizens to feel sorry for scabrous little Jimmy.

It's all too easy to forget just how worthy of his rage Bobby's targets actually were, and also how extremely hard they were to hit: in fact until the committee and Bobby waded in, it was considered impossible to make a dent in either outfit. The labor movement as such would have been a formidable opponent enough, but the Teamsters were so tough that even the labor movement could do nothing with them. As the one union that could paralyze the whole country with a single coast-to-coast strike, it was deemed untouchable: you didn't attack it, you dealt with it (a policy which subsequent presidents would return to with relief). So to take on its very tsar, first Dave Beck, and then, for three senatorial years and three more in the Justice Department, the powerhouse Jimmy Hoffa, in open combat, took at *least* a vendetta, not to mention a ton of personal courage—which probably is easier to maintain when you're angry.

But Bobby wasn't simply out to get one man, which isn't the business of Senate committees anyway: he wanted to hold up Hoffa as a horrible example of the crying need for union democracy. During this same period, his fellow committeeman and, perchance, brother, Jack Kennedy, was helping to draft the landmark Landrum-Griffin Act, which is still the

---

*Teddy's occasional slowness in public exchanges has misled people into suspecting stupidity. But according to an unimpeachable source, Teddy can be perfectly bright and articulate in private: he simply suffers from the family vice, shyness in public—a strange vice indeed for such a political family.

Teddy Kennedy, who had decided to seek the Senate seat vacated by his brother Jack, won the primary against House Speaker John McCormack's nephew Eddie and then went on to defeat Republican George Cabot Lodge, son of Henry Cabot Lodge, a near replay of Jack's own Senate campaign.

handiest weapon workers have against potential Hoffas everywhere. So both in the Senate and later as Attorney General, it was imperative for Bobby to make a test case of Jimmy Hoffa, first to prove that the Act was needed (and was not anti-labor) and second that it worked. He did both triumphantly, and by 1968 old-line union members were among his staunchest supporters. It seems that Hoffa had embarrassed *them* all along too.

The Teamsters were, as indicated, tough; but at least they had a name and address; the Mafia by contrast were and are a complete will-o'-the-wisp with several false names and thousands of addresses. Every now and then, a thug materializes in court and we think we've got something: but it's never enough. The organization itself, if that word is not too substantial for it, floats off every time into impure air. Bobby in the end could no more succeed in nailing it for good than Thomas E. Dewey and other famous Mafia-busters had: but it taught him some lessons that may have come in handy when Jack became president.

There's an old Mafia boast that "Someday we'll have a man in the White House and he won't even know it," and the sainted Frank Sinatra, who worked his heart out at the

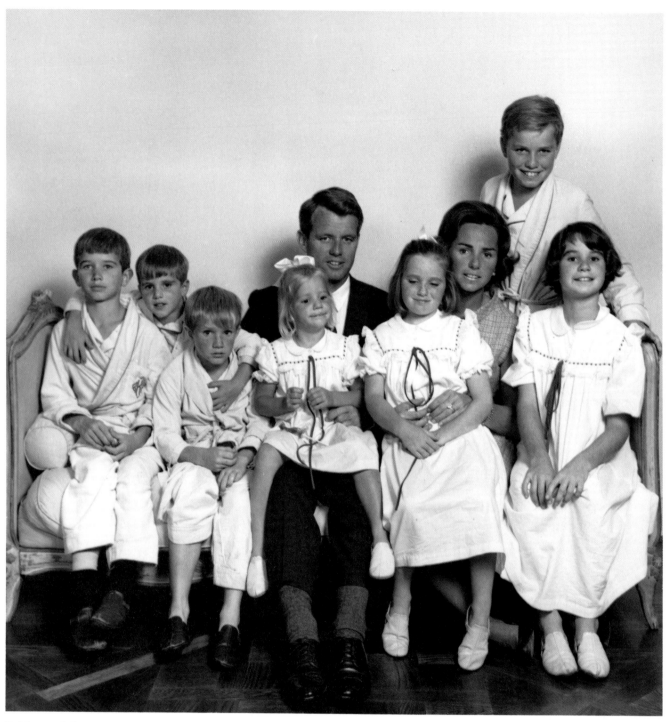

Bobby and family at the end of a Christmas-card photo session.

inauguration gala, must have seemed like the Playboy Club key to the new tenant's front, or back, door. Sinatra seems to have fascinated the silly side of Jack, and when Frank introduced him to the gorgeous Judith Campbell Exner, sometime mistress to Sam Giancana, the famous Mafia hotshot, the boys must have felt that their dream had come at least half-true: at least they had a *woman* in the White House for perhaps a few hours, although it's hard to believe that Kennedy didn't know exactly what she was.

Anyhow, that's as far as the boys ever got. With Bobby at Justice, there was no easy way to use Exner to blackmail Jack without lethal reprisals, and if the CIA *did* later use the Mafia in one of its madcap Castro-assassination plots, it's hard to say who was taking advantage of whom on that: such shenanigans certainly don't need an Exner to explain them. The subsequent disappointment which the Mafia felt for Kennedy may be judged by the distance which Sinatra later flung himself, or was flung, from everything the brothers stood for. To go from liberal Democrat to Spiro Agnew Republican is quite some leap, suggesting a veritable paroxysm of pique on Frank's part. But, of course, Frank must have assumed it was all Bobby's fault. He was, as usual, Jack's lightning conductor, and even the villains preferred it that way.

Any way you tell it, though, the Exner affair was perhaps the single most indefensible thing that President Jack ever did, and one likes to imagine Bobby assuming the older brother role for an evening to tell him so in his most biting, earnest voice (well, it's a nice picture). The trouble seems to have been that that particular side of Jack's life had become almost pure fantasy to him, completely unconnected from his real work. But at least, with or without Bobby's advice, there were no more outrageous indiscretions after Exner.

But of course, Bobby had far too much else to do than to spend his time monitoring his brother's antics: Jack knew better than to endanger his presidency again, and friends agree that he would even have taken a vow of celibacy if that's what it took. As for Bobby, on

his own he had seemed at times like an uncontrolled electrical charge, liable to go off in almost anybody's face: but now he seemed to know exactly what to do. For instance, from the first Bay of Pigs debates onward (in which he had weighed in decisively against air cover and full U.S. involvement), Bobby took it upon himself to keep a weather eye on the CIA, which might not be *quite* accountable to the Justice Department but was supposed to be so to the president himself. Here, as in other cases, Bobby's unique position as president's brother *cum* Attorney General enabled him to ride herd over this rogue outfit about as well as it could be rode herd over, although it still had its moments, especially in anything remotely related to Castro.

Equally worthy of Bobby's ramping energies was his own nominal employee, J. Edgar Hoover, the Grand Sachem of the FBI and the man "no president could fire." The Kennedys certainly had it in mind to fire J. Edgar eventually, although his own legend in the heartland would have been at least a match for theirs. But the immediate priority was simply to keep him from wrecking the civil-rights movement single-handed through the use of FBI stooges and illegal tapes, even as our Number One Cop was going through the motions of appearing to *serve* the Justice Department.

For a while a rumor was widely circulated, to the point of becoming gospel, that Bobby himself had actually authorized tapes of Martin Luther King's nighttime doings—which if so would place him squarely under the thumb of J. Edgar, instead of the other way around, and make him a co-saboteur of his own civil rights program. But the story died at last of sheer unbelievability. Bobby did authorize wire *taps* (not tapes) on King's *phone* calls to prove to the director what Bobby knew already, that King was no Communist. After that, Hoover went ahead on his own and got his own squalid tapes (illegally) anyway, to add to his trove, smaller only than the Vatican archives, of blackmail-worthy material. But all that finally counts is that he never got to use it, and King was able to complete his mission harassed but unhumiliated.

On a broader scale, Bobby's stewardship as Attorney General is said to have revved up the Justice Department as it has seldom been revved before. There was no "dead hand of the law" about it: this was clearly the president's own will, acted out at lightning speed by a hands-on manager who could cut through bureaucracy as if it wasn't there, and whose only sin was occasional arbitrariness, and not the usual inertia.

Bobby's energy proved contagious, and for a while the Kennedy can-do spirit actually crept into that most unlikely of buildings—a model of what a cabinet officer might achieve if by some miracle he both loved his work and knew his people. Yet Victor Navasky's fine book on the subject was aptly named *Kennedy Justice*, not *Bobby Justice*. Because Bobby's justice *was* Jack's, just as several of Jack's own policies were partly Bobby's. In joining his brother, Bobby had gone from being loose electricity in search of an outlet to perhaps his true destiny: being one half of a great president.

The effect was a streamlining, or purifying, of function, rarely seen (and rarely trusted) in democratic government. Nowadays we take for granted the two-falls-out-of-three school of decision-making as practiced by a Rogers and a Kissinger, or a Brzezinski and a Vance, or even a George Shultz and a whole National Security Council. That's how policy is born these days: whoever walks out of the room on his feet gets to call it.

Kennedy, by contrast, was virtually his own Secretary of State—he expressly wanted Dean Rusk to be no more than a messenger boy, although he proved a little more than that—and his adviser of last resort was most often Bobby, with whom he'd been conferring since childhood. With this nucleus of conviction at the heart of his administration, he felt free to pack his cabinet with the strongest, most independent-minded counselors he could get his hands on: the more opinions the merrier. But the buck really did stop with Jack. There was no muddy talk in those days about decision-making processes or managerial styles, which

Bobby Kennedy's position in the administration was perhaps the most difficult and certainly the most stressful. As Attorney General, he dealt with the divisive and most explosive issues of the civil rights revolt, and in the criminal justice field he had declared war on organized crime. As the president's brother, he was also his most intimate adviser. He found his release from these responsibilities at home with his family. Here, during the summer of 1962, in Hyannis Port, his time is spent with his children. Young David, who watched his father's assassination on television upstairs in the hotel where the horrible event took place, and who later was to meet a tragic death himself, was always at his side or climbing all over him.

make it impossible even to *trace* the buck. (When Reagan chivalrously claims it, how can he be really sure?)

What Bobby probably gave Jack was not in the last resort so much ideas, of which he already had more than he could use, but reassurance. Consider, Jack's body had utterly failed him once and could fail him again, and he suffered further excruciating pain in the cause of proving how healthy he was. Anyone who has had his own vulnerability spelled out for him so starkly has to suffer *some* moments of uncertainty, no matter how much willpower he hurls back at them. And indeed, most of Jack's mistakes were bred in indecisiveness, not arrogance.

What value, at such moments, might a man not then place on a friend he could *totally* trust, one whose advice could invariably be counted on to be in your interest and not his, and whose boundless energy could always be tapped into when your own appeared to flicker? There is no need to sentimentalize the relationship—the brothers themselves certainly didn't: but it must surely be a unique one in presidential annals, in which brothers have tended to play a malign role if any and wives have simply not been trained to play that kind of role at all. (A doting relative is not of much help if *all* he or she does is dote.) "I need Bobby," said Jack as soon as he became president, and the remark still resonates in a hundred ways.

Anyway, all that was over. To paraphrase Dean Acheson's famous remark about Great Britain after the war, Bobby had lost a brother but hadn't found a role. The Civil Rights Act of 1964 crowned his work as Attorney General, and even if Jack had lived, Bobby would probably have wanted to try his hand at something else—maybe the Defense or State Department, according to Ted Sorensen. Now that he had acquired the legal experience Jack once joked about, perhaps it was time for some diplomacy.

As it was, he formed the madcap scheme of applying for the vice presidency under Lyndon Johnson. Although one cannot pretend to read the labyrinthine mind of Lyndon, at least a couple of obvious motives spring to mind to explain why this particular version of the Odd Couple never ran. Bobby's Justice Department had pursued LBJ's corrupt little pal Bobby Baker with its usual zest only a year before, and Lyndon took things like that personally. And besides, why would he want to see the glittering name of Kennedy on the same billboard with his? Obviously, even a relatively mellowed Vice President Bobby would not be content for long with visiting state funerals or greeting our less significant Third World leaders: having Bobby in the next office would be like trying to raise a raccoon as a pet. And LBJ had quite enough social and

Jackie passing the Republican honor guard at the Élysée Palace in Paris.

Jack Kennedy and General de Gaulle at a state dinner at the Élysée Palace.

regional insecurities of his own without inviting the hyperactive King of the Cambridge Set on board.

Whatever his reasons, LBJ did an impressively thorough job of declining Bobby's services. After a retaliatory game of cat and mouse (the way he felt the Kennedys had toyed with *him* in 1960), he not only chose the more malleable Hubert Humphrey over Bobby but leaked the contents of the private conversation in which Bobby had asked for the job in the first place, and in general did everything else that came to mind to block a last-minute pro-Bobby surge at the 1964 convention in Atlan-

tic City. (Although Bobby did steal the show anyway, with the help of an overwhelming Jack Kennedy retrospective documentary, he did not steal the votes.)

For all that, Kennedy, as we can now call him, was heartily congratulating himself within a year on his good luck in escaping the world's most foolish job. Instead he had up and run for the Senate as a late-blooming New Yorker, and despite scattered howls of "carpetbagger," got the job. Although the wily Johnson had swiftly cut his losses by coming to New York to campaign for his dear old pal Bobby, it was too little and too late. Kennedy now had his

Jackie was the toast of Paris when the president took his first trip abroad.

own power base and was beholden to no man, as he would show in spades in 1968.

Looking back on that particular Senate race, I would have to say that Bobby's last name, and perhaps that voice, must have provided the winning margin. Because, as if to offset these advantages, he was surely one of the worst natural campaigners ever to play the game, with a tight little smile that blinked on and off meaninglessly (like his father's before him, I believe) and a simple hand gesture, up and down, up and down, which seemed to be worked by a spring. Where Jack's slight shyness had been immensely winning, Bobby's massive case was just embarrassing.

Still, it was good for Kennedy to meet the world in a non-adversarial way, and inch by sweating inch he began to relax a little. I don't know precisely the moment when it occurred to him to shoot the works, and not only to rip off his jacket but loosen his tie jauntily, but by 1968, this had transformed him into a very effective speaker indeed, in the style of an old-style union leader hollering "strike."

But then by 1968, Bobby also knew a little better what he wanted. As a working senator, he was much more conscientious than Jack and proportionately a touch more effective,

though still some distance short of what Teddy the tortoise would someday become. At any rate, his office soon hummed with life as his Justice Department had. But the Senate remained one of the few sanctuaries in the United States where being a Kennedy did not, in itself, make you anything special: you still had to make it with the Club, the Good Old Boys, and at this, Bobby proved only so-so. Unlike Jack, he was rather a special taste to begin with. And in his prosecuting days, he had managed to irk a good many other politicians besides Johnson. (This, incidentally, might have come back to haunt him fatally, if his presidential campaign of 1968 had been allowed to play itself out; but right now, it was only a minor inconvenience.)

The fact is that Bobby's mission in the Senate was not primarily legislative anyway. What the picture gave him was an incomparable platform on which, as Jack's heir, he was in a perfect position to fashion himself into a sort of tribune of the people and spokesman for the speechless—the blacks, the Chicanos, and the just plain poor. These were the years when the Great Society not only went into place but began, almost as quickly, to unravel, in a snarl of black riots, welfare scandals, and

President Kennedy at the Élysée Palace reception. He was in his prime and enjoyed himself immensely.

FOLLOWING PAGES: The young president, stopping in Paris on his first trip abroad, spent nearly eight hours, spread over three days, in intimate conversation with Charles de Gaulle. Kennedy had quipped to a reporter that "I wasn't recalled to office as my country's savior," but de Gaulle had heaped praise on JFK, calling him "a true statesman," and the two men parted with great mutual esteem for each other. Here, de Gaulle, President Kennedy, and nearly the entire French government assemble in a downpour to lay a wreath at the eternal flame under the Arc de Triomphe.

But Bobby, it turned out, could give them plenty. In 1966, he undertook two ventures, both slightly off the usual U.S. senator's beat—one close to hand in Brooklyn, where the local leaders and representatives notoriously prefer to believe that they can handle absolutely anything that needs doing around here without help from celebrity senators, and the other in California, where New Yorkers might be felt to have no business at all—and in each he proved that he could not only talk to minorities, one-on-one in crowds, but that in return he seemed to be trusted by them as no white man had been trusted in years.

all-round Vietnam-inspired anarchy. At each of these stages, in fair weather and foul, the underdog had to be championed by someone—and preferably by someone the underdog trusted.

This was perhaps the real tragedy of Lyndon Johnson. No matter how he plied the minorities with gifts, like some wealthy, desperate suitor, he could not persuade them of his sincerity, let alone his love. The Watts upheavals left this master politician in genuine perplexed distress. What *more* could he give these people? "Nothing, honey," seemed to be the answer rumbling and billowing out of the ghetto.

Kennedy's meeting with Khrushchev was fraught with frustrations. The blustering Soviet premier was full of threats, including the threat to seize Berlin, which Kennedy had been expecting and had been told by de Gaulle to ignore.

The first case was Bedford-Stuyvesant in Brooklyn (commonly known as Bed-Stuy), a largely black community, which seemed to run through the eleven o'clock news every night screaming; no one could do anything about it, and no one would let anyone else do anything about it either. Bobby's role in helping to turn this hellhole into a model community was graphically described to us by representatives of each camp, a black militant and a white businessman respectively, both of whom attested to Kennedy's rare gift for communicating effectively with blacks without losing the white man's ear.

His second venture, as a sort of senator to the nation that year, was a visit to Cesar Chavez's striking grape pickers, with whom he wished to identify himself as publicly as possible; and in a couple of pages Senor Chavez's own words will be piped in here to give you some idea of just how that meeting worked out. I can only say for myself that I wish I'd heard those words a little sooner.

Because in 1968, I was a rapid supporter of Eugene McCarthy, and from that somewhat lofty vantage point I couldn't see that Bobby's sincerity and love of minorities went that much deeper than the sanctimonious Lyndon's. The truth of the matter is that we McCarthyites were just plain sore at Bobby that year and weren't giving him much credit for anything. If you recall the circumstances: Gene McCarthy had agreed to be *the* Democratic peace candidate that year, running at risk against his own party's president; but several other potential kamikazes had been approached first, including most notably Bobby. All had declined, and then sat back curiously to watch as the flaky Minnesotan walked out alone to the end of his limb. McCarthy, of course, did surprisingly well in New Hampshire, losing by a respectably close margin, and Bobby changed his mind, quickly though with misgivings, and decided to be a peace candidate after all.*

Whatever the pros and cons of the decision (and the biggest pro turned out to be correct: McCarthy couldn't win the big ones), the timing was well-nigh fatal. McCarthy's Kids, a bunch of young activists who had stormed New Hampshire the way kids once used to storm things for Jack Kennedy, were still in the very midst of whooping it up over their mini-miracle in the snow when, at least as they saw it, this slick little specimen moved in like an old city boss to announce he was taking over the show, as if by Divine Right. Kennedy willfulness rampant. ("Bobby's a lot like me." Father Joe.)

From then on, Bobby could do nothing right with us: although his camp frequently approached us (bumped into us in bars might be closer to it), asking us to "come on over," McCarthy's (by now famous) Kids would have none of it, although Bobby coveted them for the brief rest of his days. The truth is we were already too much in love with our new leader to think straight about his rival. So you can imagine just how sincere Bobby's hectic last-minute (or so we thought) courtship of the minorities looked to the likes of us.

I happened to be in California at the time of Bobby's last primary, campaigning fitfully

---

*Bobby's ardent espousal of the peace cause may still be our best clue as to what Jack would have done in that second term.

Khrushchev was totally taken by "Jahkee," and when he was asked to shake hands with Jack at this state affair at Schönbrunn Palace he glanced at Jackie and asked to shake her hand first.

---

for Gene, so it is with all the fair-mindedness of the other guy's speech writer that I can only report that, at the time, Bobby's "compassion" seemed awfully stagey to me and us. Bobby couldn't seem to pass a poor Mexican church without flinging himself on his knees, with a cameraman hot on his heels. Could this really be Bobby, the well-known hit man? Tell it to the Marines.

Watching Kennedy's assassination on a TV set in the Hollywood Hilton just a few floors above the kitchen of horrors where it happened was shattering but not immediately enlightening. My own anti-Bobby speeches were still too fresh in my mind, though beginning then and there to turn rancid. The casual overstatements and vilifications of a campaign can seem criminal when something like this happens. But does that prove them completely wrong?

It was only years later that I realized three crucial things about all this. The first was that Bobby's courtship of minorities was *not* in the least last-minute: in 1968, he was merely touching up some old friendships. And the second was that Bobby's love of these people *had* to be enacted stagily from the word "go." The tempered words of a Eugene McCarthy would in the end have won him no more black trust than LBJ's magnolia-dripping approach had. This was not Harvard Yard, and these

were not divinity students. Then too, it may have been particularly essential for a shy man like Bobby to make a display of himself, even, indeed, going down on his knees—all this depending, though, on the third thing I realized, which is that the staginess has to ring true with its intended audience; it has, if you like, to be sincere staginess.

On this point, I have received reassurance from innumerable sources. Everyone I have talked to who knew Bobby intimately swears that his love of the downtrodden was absolutely genuine, and that they (the downtrodden) knew it. One witness, not at all given to sentimentality, remembers Bobby holding the hand of a dying old lady for an endless length of time, as if he couldn't bear to let go: and there wasn't a camera within miles. And other people, other stories.

However this kind of naked compassion may have played in New York, which is always on the lookout for corn and finding it, Bobby seems to have worked some sort of miracle on the spot. But this is something we could have learned ourselves from Cesar Chavez back in 1966, if we'd been paying attention. The following excerpt, taken from his oral history in the Library of Congress, begins with a startling comparison between Bobby and his charismatic brother Jack:

"Oh . . . Jack Kennedy had a real good recception among the minorities, but nothing like Bobby, no. They had all this respect and admiration for John . . . but they looked at him as sort of the minority kind of person himself . . . with Bobby it was like an entirely different kind of thing . . . it was like he was one of ours."

Read it and blink. Are we sure he's got the names in the right order? *Bobby* more appealing that *Jack?* Yes indeed, it seems that for a few golden moments he actually was, and by a mile. "For every man working for John Kennedy [in 1960]," says Chavez, "we must have had about fifty men working for Bobby. It was electrifying. . . . This line is very seldom crossed. It was like respect, admiration, love, idolized. God. I can't explain

it." Chavez breaks off, uncharacteristically lost for words.

Thus it would seem that by sheer force of will and conviction, the shy, surly younger brother had crashed the class barrier to become the one thing Jack could never quite make, "one of ours" to America's workers. In this incandescent phase, the hard-bitten Bobby was actually perceived by these people as several kinds of savior. Chavez says that to the old people, he seemed like a bishop on a visit, while to the young ones, he gave off a hot celebrity charge "like John Kennedy as *president*" (my italics). In both cases, religious imagery recurs. "The amazing thing," says Chavez, "was that he could turn everybody on . . . sure, there are people who are ad-

Upon arriving in London on a personal visit, Jack first went to 10 Downing Street to pay his respects to Macmillan.

mired, but there's a reserve, you know, they'll just go so far. But this was, no, this was just like there's no limit to the . . ." words fail him again—possibly because they don't exist. It was as though, once Bobby had broken down his own formidable reserves, he found himself, for the first and last time, loved unreservedly and wantonly in return.

No doubt, if Bobby had lived, the California primary campaign would have found its way into the files under "miscellaneous episodes." There would have been other campaigns in other states, few of which reported in as particularly heavy on migrant farm workers or Mexican Americans, and Bobby would presumably have gone back to being a more conventional candidate. But in the shocking light of his murder, the California adventure takes on the nature of a final pilgrimage, his own road to Golgotha, and everything he did along the way becomes a significant act of witness. So it suddenly seems tremendously moving and right that he should have spent his next-to-last hours on earth talking as he had never talked before to the poor and the dispossessed, his last consuming and consummating passions.

One doesn't have to believe in predestination to feel that in some sense this was what his life had been about all along, and that that death henceforth would serve principally to direct our eyes toward it. For those few weeks at least Bobby became a very great man, transcending his own nature and even some of our own quibbles about it.

And yet to the end we still accused him of showboating. On the day he died a reporter on the McCarthy floor of the Hilton observed that "compared with this guy [Bobby], Jack was all heart." Thus grudgingly do we admit to the smallest changes in our fixed images. I now believe that the only real proof we ever needed of Bobby's sincerity was the fact that he was willing to risk the charge of showboating in the first place. It must have taken a terrific act of will for this very private man to let his emotions consume him so openly, while the cynics looked on from the press bus.

He also must have felt it was worth doing in itself, because there was precious little political capital in it for him. All the latest insider surveys indicated that the backlash against the Great Society and the Lost Children of the Sixties had propelled the electorate into a thoroughly Dayton, Ohio, frame of mine. So there weren't many votes in the underdog that year. And if Bobby had continued to campaign, as I'm sure he would have, on the latter's behalf, he might have had a sticky time of it. Because reports out of Dayton were particularly agreed on one thing, which was that the underdog had received more than enough help already.

At this point, it becomes as painful as it is inevitable to speculate on whether Bobby, had he lived, could have won the presidency in 1968 anyway. At the time, he was still considered quite the long shot, despite his name. On the Democratic side of the fence, the McCarthyites remained as implacable as ever. As I remember, we were particularly tired of hearing how much Bobby had "grown," partly because this overall explanation had been worked to death by the other team to erase Richard Nixon's latest sins (remember all the

In London, President Kennedy and Jackie stayed at 4 Buckingham Palace, the home of Lee Radziwill, Jackie's sister. Jack was to be the godfather of Lee's new baby as well as the guest of honor at a reception attended by a small, elite group. Here, Jack, then the most powerful man in the Western world, is sitting in the foyer of Lee's house, perusing the papers and waiting for the guests to arrive. Pierre Salinger, his press aide, is with him.

new Nixons?'), and it was only much later that we realized how radically different Bobby was from all those other "growing" politicians. As for the Hubert Humphrey people, they already seemed so certain they had the 1968 nomination locked up, Bobby or no Bobby, that they didn't even deign to enter their man in any primaries whatever.* They must have assumed that insofar as Kennedy and McCarthy were factors at all, they were self-canceling ones who would spend the rest of a long exhausting summer knocking each other out.

But that was only one side of the picture. On the other was the famous Kennedy dynamic. Bobby was visibly beginning to roll, and not just among single-issue voters. He had already run surprisingly well in the suburbs of Indiana and Nebraska, which was considered enemy territory, and California itself hadn't been all Chicanos by any means: the right-wing denizens of Orange County also seemed to like what they saw and, for a peace candidate, Bobby seemed to go over uncommonly well with blue-collar voters too, maybe because he didn't have all those McCarthy col-

lege kids yapping at his ankles. In fact, Bobby's bizarre blue-collar appeal was rapidly turning into a swing factor in the campaign.

And then there was the good old Kennedy machine, still at the height of its powers, and straining at the leash to move in on Chicago, which was definitely its kind of town. Mayor Daley was, as you'll recall, a confirmed Kennedy man, and we would have had a very different sort of convention from the nightmare we wound up with. A peace candidate with blue-collar appeal and without attendant yippies was the only kind of peace candidate for Dick Daley, and Bobby might even have entered the city like a conquering general, all set to cut his way through the remaining flab of the old Democratic Party. The cautious forces hunkered around Hubert Humphrey might, if so, have found their hands full to overflowing trying to resist this dynamo, who was, to top it off, not only infinitely more glamorous but much more professional than they and their candidate were.

It would have been a wonderful convention to witness; in fact, of all the events in history that never happened, this may be the one I miss most—this, and its aftermath. I am supposing here that the self-confidence Bobby had picked up along the way would have grown

*That was something that you could do in those days and get away with it. Hubert Humphrey's success in doing it that year is one of the reasons you can't get away with it now.

at each whistle stop and that the late-blooming charisma, which Chavez's downtrodden clients had recognized and celebrated, would not have remained confined to them for long; journalists tell me you could sense it in the club car, a feeling of mission, of a life-work exploding.

And up against this elemental force, we would have had exactly what? A chatterbox of a vice president who didn't feel quite free to speak out just yet, a brilliant eccentric named McCarthy whose constituency was still mostly in the street and the classrooms, and behind them both the brooding spirit of a lame-duck giant—well, it would have been a darling convention, as they say in Dublin.

And then, so long as we're dreaming about this, we might have gone on to witness the piquant spectacle of Richard Nixon confronted with yet another Kennedy that fall. For this surreal contest, Bobby might have found himself backed by two crack regiments from the old Roosevelt coalition, which experts had assured us could never be put together again: the racial minorities and the white blue-collars. And who knows what else? Insofar as Bobby could persuade the world to accept him as Jack's true heir and earthly delegate, he had at his fingertips forces beyond the reach of everyday politics: for instance, if he wanted to end the war in Vietnam, it wasn't

like some trendy liberal senator wanting to end it—this was a *Kennedy*; and if he called for a renewal on the waning era of selfless sacrifice, he had the mandate for that too. (The first sprouts of the "me generation" were certainly not going to sacrifice for anything *less* than a Kennedy.) The idealism of the sixties had all but guttered out by then for want of a leader, and a new cycle of self-interest was on its way, but the Bobby of 1968 might just have got the fire going again, with results that are almost too tantalizing to think about.

In fact, a Bobby Kennedy presidency remains a wonderfully rich subject to conjure with; but that's all we can do with it. Because in place of a truly triumphal inauguration, what we had to settle for was Bobby's last, slow, tragic return to Washington in a funeral train. For hundreds of miles, Americans lined the tracks, two- to ten- to infinity-deep, to watch the train pass, and weep inconsolably over it, like the Women of Troy. And that incredible turnout was as close to a national mandate as Bobby was ever permitted to get. However, for a devout Christian like Bobby, the blood of martyrs is always the seed for something greater, and he himself had come as close to proving it as one man could in his reaction to Jack's death. Surely his own blood deserves no less.

TOP: On his way to the crypt at London's Catholic Westminster Cathedral, where the baptism was to take place, Kennedy pauses to shake hands with some nuns.

BOTTOM: Jack as godfather.

Yet, for all the tragedy in their lives, a funeral note does not really suit the Kennedys, especially at the end of a book about them. I prefer to think of the two brothers in their eternal prime, still looking quizzically at us from photographs, still telling us plenty.

Having begun this meditation announcing grandly that there can be only one great man to a family, I find myself now wondering at times which one it was, or rather how, exactly, the greatness was distributed. It would be too simple, as such statements inevitably are, to call Jack and Bobby respectively the head and heart, the intellect and will, of a great presidency, because each was more than a bit of both. But a Bobby presidency might have proved a touch more abrasive than Jack's: owing to his sheer intensity, some people might have perceived him, against his most express wishes, as perennially leading one half of the country against the other,* while Jack without Bobby might have seemed a shade Hamlet-like at

*In the language of Marshall McLuhan, the presidency is a "hot medium" like TV, requiring a cool performer, and Bobby might have just have blown out a tube.

times, as he saw just too many sides to too many questions.

But together they made, to my mind, an extraordinary president. No leader in so cumbersome a polity as ours should ever be judged for keeps on the strength of slightly less than three years in office. But if the last word on that dazzling interruption to our normal ways still has to be no better than "promising" (I'd hold out for more than that myself), it was at least that in abundance: and the promise is still there, like some quality in the air, for anyone with the wit and vitality to use it.

There has been so much stress laid recently on the impossible burdens of the modern presidency that one grows exhausted just from reading about it: but perhaps this is simply the result of watching too many people who aren't quite up to it, intellectually or psychologically, grimly grappling with it. As an antidote to all this presidential fatigue, theirs and ours, imagine for a moment the two brothers hitting town as for the first time and pouring zestfully over the current (never mind which) president's agenda—and take heart.

Jack with baby Caroline in Hyannis Port in 1958.

Acknowledgments

The authors wish to thank Steve Smith, chairman of Joseph P. Kennedy Enterprises, Inc., for his generous help in arranging interviews, supplying documents, and contributing his own valuable insights into the Kennedy years; Dick Goodwin, formerly of the Kennedy White House staff, for his thoughts on the Alliance for Progress; Ben Bradlee, editor-in-chief of the *Washington Post*, for illuminating the private Jack and Bobby; and the Kennedy Library staff for arranging interviews with a group of Boston public-school teenagers, who revealed to us some of the generation's thoughts about the Kennedy legacy.

We also wish to thank Franklin Thomas, now president of the Ford Foundation and former head of Bobby Kennedy's Bedford-Stuyvesant project; Benno Schmidt, chairman of J. H. Whitney and Company, who contributed so much time and care to that same project; musician Peter Yarrow, of Peter, Paul and Mary; and Eugene Mihaesco, the brilliant Romanian artist who was so deeply affected by President Kennedy's death, for their interviews.

We are grateful to Michael Beschloss for reading an important stretch of the manuscript and adding some corrections and clarifications.

We offer our apologies to Theodore Sorensen for borrowing his title *The Kennedy Legacy*. Our only excuse for this is that Mr. Sorensen had coined the exact right phrase for what we wanted to talk about, and any variation on it, such as "The Kennedy Inheritance" or "Heritage," seemed to us clumsy and imprecise. Incidentally, the Sorensen book remains simply indispensable—and not just for its title.

Michael Fragnito of Viking Penguin deserves our gratitude for believing in this book so strongly, and so does Barbara Williams, our editor.

The excellent prints of the photographs were made by Mike Kirkorian of Modernage and Phil Vance of Photo Vision. Bill Gott did the retouching where needed. To these people, as well as to typist Barbara Hill, our sincere thanks.